Understanding
Ceremony

Understanding
Ceremony

A STUDENT CASEBOOK TO ISSUES, SOURCES, AND HISTORICAL DOCUMENTS

Lynn Domina

The Greenwood Press
"Literature in Context" Series
Claudia Durst Johnson, Series Editor

GREENWOOD PRESS
Westport, Connecticut • London

Library of Congress Cataloging-in-Publication Data

Domina, Lynn.
Understanding *Ceremony* : a student casebook to issues, sources, and historical documents /
Lynn Domina.
    p. cm. — (The Greenwood Press "Literature in context" series, ISSN 1074-598X)
Includes bibliographical references.
ISBN 0-313-32859-5
1. Silko, Leslie, 1948- Ceremony—Handbooks, manuals, etc. 2. Indians in literature—
Handbooks, manuals, etc. I. Title. II. Series.
    PS3569.I44C43 2004
    813'.54—dc22   2004017862

British Library Cataloguing in Publication Data is available.

Library of Congress Catalog Card Number: 2004017862
ISBN: 0–313–32859–5
ISSN: 1074–598X

First published in 2004

Greenwood Press, 88 Post Road West, Westport, CT 06881
An imprint of Greenwood Publishing Group, Inc.
www.greenwood.com

Printed in the United States of America

The paper used in this book complies with the
Permanent Paper Standard issued by the National
Information Standards Organization (Z39.48–1984).

10   9   8   7   6   5   4   3   2   1

Contents

Acknowledgments

Numerous people have contributed to the success of this project. First, I want to thank Lynn Araujo of Greenwood Press and Claudia Johnson, series editor, for inviting me to write this book. My colleagues at the State University of New York (SUNY)—Delhi provide evidence daily that academics can be pleasant and sane people. Kathryn DeZur in particular has listened to many of my moans and groans, offered solutions to insoluble problems, and kept me on task during our Friday morning "accountability coffees." Anna Reed has fielded dozens of interlibrary loan requests more cheerfully and efficiently than any faculty member deserves. Diane Block of the Museum of New Mexico went beyond the call of duty in assisting me with photo reproductions. Philip Red Eagle and Art Shedd graciously afforded me several hours of their time, and I would have been introduced to neither of them were it not for Janet McAdams and Candace Vancko. Finally, during the most important hours of my day, Sandra and Amy cheer my soul.

Introduction

Leslie Marmon Silko's *Ceremony* is among the handful of novels by Native American writers most frequently taught in high school and college literature courses. First published in 1977, *Ceremony* is one of the texts that gave rise to the term "Native American Renaissance" following the publication of N. Scott Momaday's *House Made of Dawn* a decade earlier. If consensus could be reached on a canon of contemporary Native American literature, Silko's work would certainly be included, along with that of Momaday, Louise Erdrich, James Welch, Linda Hogan, and others. *Ceremony* is taught not simply in Native American surveys but also in American literature, contemporary literature, and American studies courses, as well as courses on the novel.

The most prominent thematic issue in *Ceremony* concerns the efficacy of traditional healing ceremonies, especially for individuals whose conditions are the result of compound trauma. Tayo suffers from battle fatigue not only because of what he witnessed during the war but also because of all he had experienced before. He lives at a particular historical moment, one that has arrived after centuries of oppression and suppression of native traditions through European encounter. Related to the conflict between traditional healing practices and modern Western medicine is an implicit conflict between European and Native American cultures, generally. The novel undermines this simple opposition, however, by opposing good to evil instead and by overtly refusing to align good with Native and evil with European. Most of the honorable and admirable characters, in fact, are of mixed race.

The novel is set in the years following World War II, and the war provides part of the back story. Because Tayo has served in the Pacific and been captured by the Japanese, and because Laguna is so close to the test site of the atomic bomb, Silko is able to link the war and its aftermath to mythic stories that explain the release of evil upon the world. The most modern—and hor-rifying—of technologies, in other words, are re-enactments of stories that have been unfolding for millennia.

Tayo's own background, revealed through flashbacks, illustrates several prob-lems affiliated with contemporary Native American life, especially poverty and alcohol abuse, which also occurs among Tayo and his friends. A prerequisite of Tayo's healing is his sobriety. In contrast to other veterans who create their own rituals around drunken behavior, Tayo chooses another mode of behav-ior, and this choice saves him.

This book begins with a literary analysis, focusing on *Ceremony*'s emergent themes and its mixed-genre nature. Chapters 2 and 3 situate the novel his-torically. Chapter 2 focuses on the history and cultures of Pueblo people and of Laguna specifically, while chapter 3 examines issues related to World War II. Included here are not only transcripts of legal proceedings and excerpts from government reports but also interviews recorded specifically for this book. Chapter 4 compares the value systems and ethical concerns raised by tradi-tional Native belief systems and conventional Western medicine. Finally, chap-ter 5 analyzes the role of alcohol and other social problems within Native communities. Each chapter concludes with a list of projects for written or oral exploration and a list of resources for further reading.

NOTE

Page numbers in parentheses refer to the Penguin edition of Leslie Marmon Silko's *Ceremony,* published in 1986.

1 ————————————————

Literary Analysis

In several interviews, Leslie Marmon Silko states, perhaps a bit disingenuously given how carefully structured the novel is, that *Ceremony* is organized as one extended narrative without chapter breaks because when she was writing the book, she didn't realize novels were conventionally divided into chapters. Whether Silko disregarded chapter breaks intentionally or inadvertently, the novel's continuous flow affects readers' reception of it. The present mingles with the near and distant past in such a way that events seem to occur concurrently; distinctions among the mythic past, the historical past, and the characters' personal situations become irrelevant, even misleading. The inappropriateness of such distinctions, in fact, contributes to the novel's themes. Because, in part, of *Ceremony*'s structure, this analysis will be organized thematically, although none of the themes exists in isolation from the others. To some extent, these themes are revealed through plot and character, but they are also conveyed through Silko's style and through the literary conventions she violates.

THE CEREMONIES IN *CEREMONY*

Several brief ceremonies occur within the novel, and Tayo completes a more extensive and complex ceremony as part of his reincorporation into his culture. In this sense, the novel is about ceremonies. Yet the novel is also itself a ceremony; its form both duplicates and exceeds its content. Within the plot, readers can point to various moments when a ceremony begins or is completed, yet after examining the entire novel, readers also understand that the ceremony began long before the novel opens and will continue long after the novel ends—if the world is to survive.

Respect for and willingness to participate in traditional ceremonies sometimes distinguishes one character from another. In contrast to Rocky, Tayo covers a killed deer's head with his jacket as a rite of hunting, honoring the deer's willingness to sacrifice itself for the good of humanity. Although he may intellectually understand scientific explanations of the universe—explanations he has been taught in school—such an understanding does not persuade him to discard his culture's traditional interpretation of humanity's role and responsibility in the world. Because Tayo accepts traditional beliefs, he is more spiritually prepared to accept his role in the continuous ceremony that regularly re-creates the earth—even if he initially agrees to the ceremony only as an attempt to restore his own health.

After Tayo has been back at Laguna for some time following the war, when it is clear to his relatives that his health is not improving and that he has been taken from them just as his mother and Rocky had been, Tayo's grandmother suggests that he needs a medicine man even if he is still physically present. The family consults Ku'oosh, who arrives at Tayo's home and begins telling a complicated story. The story seems not to originate with Ku'oosh but rather to be simply transmitted by him. Initially, Tayo doesn't understand the story's relevance, but then Ku'oosh begins to describe a cave that Tayo remembers. In times past, "they took the scalps and threw them down there. Tayo knew what the old man had come for" (35). Ku'oosh will perform a scalp ceremony for Tayo to cleanse him of the violence he had participated in during the war, a necessary act if Tayo is to be successfully reincorporated into Laguna society. Traditionally, the ceremony had marked a transition when warriors returned from battle, since their roles within the pueblo should not be tinged with destruction. Tayo suggests that Ku'oosh can help him, even though he doesn't believe he has killed any Japanese—though he is also afraid that he has killed someone without being aware of it, a mark of modern warfare. Tayo also believes that he has "done things far worse," such as cursing the flies and the rain, and that his curses have returned to curse his people (36). Perhaps the scalp ceremony will restore the harmony he destroyed while he was away at war, even if he didn't literally kill any Japanese. When Ku'oosh leaves at the conclusion of the ceremony, he expresses unease that the ceremony appears not to have cured other veterans of this war; Ku'oosh worries for the future of all the people if their ceremonies no longer function to restore harmony—for if harmony can never be restored, the destroyers will inevitably emerge as victors.

Eventually, Ku'oosh recommends, through Robert, that Tayo visit Old Betonie. Initially, Betonie's residence outside Gallup seems an odd juxtaposition.

Although from his hogan he looks down at the arroyo, recognizing daily that Native Americans in Gallup are forced to live where white people won't, he asserts that he belongs to the land he lives on. Although he keeps traditional customs and dresses in traditional styles, his hogan is filled with modern documents—calendars, phone books, newspapers—that nevertheless assist him in ceremonies, just as speaking English assists him in fulfilling his traditional role. Then Tayo notices Betonie's eyes, which are hazel like Tayo's, and Betonie acknowledges his Mexican grandmother; both Betonie and Tayo—as well as others who will be significant participants in the ceremony—have mixed-race ancestry. Such a detail, referred to at other points in the novel also, implies that individuals whose very identity represents union rather than separation are the people most necessary to restore the world; they are especially blessed.

Betonie and Tayo begin a conversation, with Betonie guiding Tayo to pertinent details—he wants to hear about Josiah's cattle and Night Swan, but he indicates that Tayo's aunt is irrelevant to the ceremony. During this conversation, Betonie suggests that Tayo's story is part of a much larger mythic story and that the ceremony Tayo will be required to complete will fulfill part of this larger story. Eventually, Betonie introduces Tayo to his assistant, Shush, who also has a mythic identity as a bear-child. Betonie and Shush perform a ceremony during which they create a sand painting around Tayo and call on the Bear People, who have the power to restore a person to himself. That night, Tayo dreams about Josiah's cattle. Later, Betonie draws Tayo a diagram of stars forming a particular pattern, and he tells Tayo to watch out for four distinct elements: the stars, a mountain, a woman, and the cattle.

Hunting for the cattle, Tayo meets a woman who eventually identifies herself as Ts'eh and who retains a traditional clothing style; that night, he notices that the stars form the pattern Betonie had drawn for him. The next morning, Tayo attempts to sing a sunrise chant, though he's uncertain of the exact words. Although he has not previously made it his habit to begin his day this way, he now feels called to pray properly, as if something greater than himself is guiding his actions. Tayo's desire here signals both the extent of Tayo's healing and the potential he has to participate in a much more significant ceremony.

Tayo continues searching for Josiah's cattle, discovering them eventually on a ranch fenced in and owned by a white man. The extended scene that follows most dramatically illustrates tension between white people, who are able to exploit the American legal system, and the assumptions that underlie it regarding individual and property rights, and Native Americans; yet even this scene also demonstrates that the primary conflict in the novel is between the forces of good and evil that only seem, sometimes, to duplicate conflicts between racial groups. Tayo cuts the rancher's fence, planning to guide the cattle back through it. During his journey, a mountain lion appears to him, and Tayo recites a poem of blessing, then sprinkles pollen into its tracks. The mountain lion will prove to be a blessing to Tayo, for he is soon spotted and captured by employees of the rancher who owns the land. They believe he has trespassed in order to poach deer and intend to deliver him to the sheriff, but one of the white men spots the mountain lion tracks and decides to release Tayo in order to hunt the mountain lion himself.

By this time, the cattle have found the hole in the fence and escaped through it. They have followed an arroyo into a dead end, a trap designed by Ts'eh, for once the cattle ran into the gulley, she slid a gate across the only opening. Several other details in the novel confirm that this woman is the one Betonie had seen when the ceremony began, and in some ways the ceremony seems complete here because Tayo has regained his health and the cattle, and he has begun to be reintegrated into his family. But his most disastrous temptation has yet to occur.

Tayo decides to live at the family's ranch for a while, away from the village. There he again meets Ts'eh. She warns him that the ceremony is not yet complete, that the destroyers hope still to win, and that Tayo will continue to play a crucial role, though people he trusts will betray him. Soon, he does meet up with Leroy and Harley, who are drunk, and while he is relieved to see his friends, he also senses that something is drastically wrong. Because Leroy and Harley are so drunk, Tayo is able to outwit them, disabling their truck and taking their screwdriver along with him so they won't be able to reconnect any wires easily. That night, he witnesses Emo and Pinkie torturing Harley, and he realizes that Harley is suffering the punishment they had planned for Tayo. Tayo fingers the screwdriver in his pocket and visualizes Emo's skull, imagining himself thrusting the screwdriver into Emo's head. He realizes, however, that his own participation in such violence would destroy the ceremony, and that witchery would emerge victorious.

Tayo returns to Laguna, where he tells his story to a group of old men in the kiva—a telling that is in itself ceremonial. The men are most interested in Ts'eh, asking, among other questions, about the color of her eyes, for she too is of mixed race. The other men respond to Tayo's story with a blessing, with a statement of belief that the people will again receive blessing. Just as the people have been cursed through Tayo's actions, now they are blessed.

The novel itself concludes with a blessing: "Sunrise / accept this offering, / Sunrise" (262). Together with the novel's opening, an assertion that the narrated events consist of Thought-Woman's thoughts, followed by a single introductory word, "Sunrise," this short poem demonstrates that the book is not simply about an extended ceremony but is also itself a ceremony. During the course of the novel, Tayo also recites these prayers as a means of participating in the larger ceremony encapsulated by the book. The book includes blessings, in other words, but also begins and ends with a blessing upon the world—a blessing spoken by an omniscient narrator rather than by any particular character. By including these chants where she does, Silko indicates that the blessings aren't simply upon the world imagined in the novel but extend beyond its covers to the world in which all readers live.

CEREMONY'S MYTHOLOGICAL WORLD

Many of the individual aspects of Tayo's ceremony, as well as other details of the novel, are dependent on Laguna mythology for their significance. Although this mythology is sometimes in conflict with other methods of interpreting the world, that conflict is a minor one, for the novel would be incoherent without its mythology. Implicitly, the world is incoherent without a mythology. (For the purposes of this analysis, "myth" is not defined simply as something that is not true; rather, a "mythology" is a system of interpretation that creates meaning about the world. Whether a myth is factually true or not is irrelevant as long as people make decisions and take actions because they believe the myth to be true.) Stories parents and grandparents pass down to subsequent generations often incorporate cultural mythology, and several of the stories Tayo has been taught interact to propel the plot and reveal many of the themes of *Ceremony*.

Early in the novel during a flashback to the war, Tayo remembers cursing the rain and the flies as he struggles to keep Rocky from dying when they are both prisoners of the Japanese. Later, he interprets his curse as reverberating on his own culture because a drought follows and hence seems to proceed from his words. Walking into a bar where a man sits with a flyswatter and where dozens of dead flies are already stuck to fly strips, Tayo remembers a story Josiah had told him as a boy. Because his teacher had told him flies carry diseases, Tayo had been proudly killing them. According to Josiah, the people had once been saved from drought-induced death because a greenbottle fly had conveyed the people's repentance to the mother of the earth. During the war, however, Tayo's anger and grief prove stronger than any prohibition against mistreating flies, and he crushes them in his hands.

The story of the greenbottle fly is only one segment of an extended-creation myth intended to teach the people their place in the world and the respect they should show other creatures. Another story, set during a time of drought, explains how a hummingbird saved the people. This story is related in several sections throughout the novel; that is, part of the myth will be narrated, and then the novel will return to the central plot of Tayo's life, then return again to another section of the hummingbird myth. When asked how he can be so well nourished, the hummingbird tells the people about worlds below their world. He reveals that the mother of the earth has grown angry with the people and instructs them in making amends to her. He offers to serve as their messenger. After several intermediary steps, the people's offering is complete, and the storm clouds return. The myth isn't complete, however, until the people hear a bit of advice not to offend their mother again. Although this particular myth can be narrated as if it is one discrete story, it exists, like many myths, within a much broader context and acquires some of its meaning from other interconnected myths. In this case for example, the mother of the people had gone away not simply because the people had neglected her, but because their neglect stemmed from distraction by a magician. A trickster figure persuades them to believe his magic is powerful enough to provide water and food; they no longer need to perform the rituals through which their mother provides sustenance.

Because Laguna is situated in such a dry climate, many of the myths concern drought. The stories explain why droughts have occurred in the past and what the people have done to bring rain. Contemporary people, remembering the myths, can study their own actions to determine how they can atone for their mistakes and save themselves. Early in *Ceremony,* immediately after the flashback in which Tayo curses the rain, a story explains how rivalry between two sisters caused another drought. Reed Woman spends her entire day bathing—and splashing water down to earth—while her sister, Corn Woman, works hard in the sun. Irritated at what she believes is an unfair division of labor, Corn Woman scolds Reed Woman, who leaves, taking the water with her. Without rain, all the animals and plants including, ironically, the corn, begin to die. All of creation is interdependent, the myth teaches, and no one will survive who offends another being.

These myths are all narrated within *Ceremony,* yet the novel itself is narrated within the larger myth of Thought-Woman, who is sometimes known as Spider Grandmother. According to the narrator, the story contained in *Ceremony* exists because Thought-Woman is thinking of the events as they occur. The description of Thought-Woman occurs in the present tense—that is, she is thinking the story now as it is being told; the situation is not that she has thought the story in the past and it is now being passed onto others as the other myths are. The narrator, who is not Thought-Woman, reveals the story orally and simultaneously with Thought-Woman's thoughts. Everything that exists, including the characters in the novel and also those of us outside the novel, comes into existence through Thought-Woman's mind.

Another of the most memorable mythic stories in the novel also features the idea that events occur because they have been thought and spoken. Language has power, not merely to describe or persuade, but also literally to create. Although the idea that language and words hold creative force can be attractive, one must also remember that destructive and evil actions are equally viable through language. The environmental and genocidal destruction of Native American cultures that has occurred since European contact is explained in another of the myths central to the novel. Exactly halfway through the book, Betonie reminds Tayo of the means by which white people were created. A group of witches had met to participate in a competition, testing their skills against each other. Some of the exploits described in the story are repulsive: "dead babies simmering in blood / circles of skull cut away / all the brains sucked out" (134). Finally, only one witch remains who hasn't demonstrated any impressive abilities. This witch begins to speak and warns the others that events will occur as they are spoken. The witch's story involves white people coming from across the ocean—white people who deny that the earth is alive—people who will be determined to destroy the world. Horrified by the language, the other witches agree that the storytelling witch has won the contest and beg that witch to recall the words. But they can't be recalled. White people have been created through language.

Although a superficial reading of this story might seem to indicate that the novel positions white people as a source of evil, Betonie reminds Tayo that evil originates with the witches, the destroyers, rather than with particular groups of people. Additionally, the story situates the Native Americans within a particular circle of power, for white people exist only by virtue of a Native American speech act. While this particular story doesn't reveal what will happen after white people begin to kill even each other, creating explosions that threaten all of the earth, other stories within the Laguna mythological system do suggest that the world will continue, that the people will be saved.

GENRE AND *CEREMONY*

Many of these mythic stories are presented in *Ceremony* through poetry rather than more conventionally through prose, a strategy that is more common in Native American writing than in the writing of other ethnic groups. In many Native American cultures, generic boundaries aren't rigidly defined, especially within texts that were originally transmitted orally. Much of the material that is formatted as poetry in *Ceremony* is itself ceremonial. To some extent, the stories revealed through poetry have a different meaning, often a more clearly sacred meaning, than those revealed through more ordinary prose. If the novel were to be read aloud, many of these poems could be chanted, while the prose would be spoken with commonplace tones and cadences.

Occasionally, the text itself directly reveals that a poem has been recited by a particular character. For example, when Tayo is traveling with Old Betonie and

Shush, the narrative seems to be interrupted by a story, set off as poetry, in which a young man has been changed into a coyote. Because his family wants him to return to his human form, they consult the bear people, who have "the power to restore the mind" (141). The bear people instruct the man's family in a ceremony, which concludes with the creation of a pollen boy, a figure created from pollen in the center of a larger corn painting. When the poem ends and the narrative returns to the present, Tayo is sitting in the center of a corn painting, and the other details of the painting correspond to those in the recited story. The juxtaposition of these details reveals that Betonie, and presumably others, believes that Tayo's mind has been lost to him, through trickery analogous to the coyote's or through a worse type of witchery. Betonie's assistant, whose name translates as Bear, makes bear prints around Tayo, and then the prose narrative and the chanting merge as Betonie and Shush teach Tayo the way home to himself and to his people. Clearly, the structure of this section of the novel reveals that the mythic stories contained in *Ceremony* aren't simply entertainments speculating about a time long ago and a place far away; they remain pertinent, even crucial, for the present, not simply because they assist the characters in interpreting the present, but because they continue to shape events in the present.

Betonie's assistant, Shush, is introduced with another poetic story, one that corresponds to yet differs in significant ways from the one affiliated with Tayo's loss of himself. When Tayo hears that "Shush" means "bear," he realizes why the boy seems peculiar. The poem that immediately follows describes a young boy who wanders away from his family. The family members follow the boy's tracks until they become mixed with bear tracks. The medicine man imitates a bear in order to appeal to the boy, just as Shush imitates a bear during the ceremony for Tayo. Eventually, the boy in the story who had become a bear returns to his human form, but he nevertheless remains not quite human, as if a part of him has remained with the bears. This story explains why Shush, too, is not quite like other children. Although this story resembles the one in which coyotes trick a man into becoming one of them, the two stories function very differently. The story of the bear concerns loss, but it's not as ominous as the coyote story. And the bear story provides a foundation for understanding bear people as healers rather than tricksters.

Only one of the sections set as poetry initially seems to contain neither ceremonial nor any other type of traditional value. It initially seems lacking in mythic significance. In the midst of the extended scene that climaxes with Tayo stabbing Emo, the narrative shifts into poetry. The veterans have created their own postwar ritual: go to a bar, get drunk, tell war stories featuring sexual encounters with white women. The same stories are often repeated; the important factor is not any new detail that might be revealed, but the act of storytelling itself. Here, Emo describes picking up two women in a bar and spending the night with both. Yet readers might ask why this story is so important that it is formatted as if it has mythic significance. Isn't it just a bit of bragging that is almost certainly embellished? Isn't it just the type of story that should be ignored, discounted, rather than enhanced in status?

Old Betonie provides one answer when he asserts that the ceremonies have been changing since they were instituted. Even if the words remain identical, even if a yellow gourd is always used in one ceremony, blue pollen in another, the pollen will be different from one painting to the next and the gourd from one generation to the next. Betonie extends this idea to suggest that as the circumstances, the particular contexts, that necessitate a ceremony change, the ceremony should adjust to acknowledge those differences. Analogously, as the lives of the people change, mythological systems must be flexible enough to incorporate contemporary lives. If the old stories no longer speak to the people, the stories will die, and according to the terms of the novel, the people will die also. So although the veterans' storytelling rituals may not be as sacred as some other ceremonies, Silko nevertheless suggests, in structuring this story as a poem, that these stories will continue to acquire meaning over time, that they will be told long after the participants are dead, that they will enter Laguna mythology at a time when World War II has receded to the vast distant past.

STORYTELLING IN *CEREMONY*

Many stories get told in *Ceremony*, including the comparatively brief yet repetitive war stories told by Harley, Emo, and other veterans. Old Betonie tells part of his story; Night Swan tells part of hers. Tayo remembers Rocky's story. Old Betonie suggests that Tayo's aunt's response to him is an unimportant part of the story. The opening page of the novel suggests that the entire narrative is a story Thought-Woman is thinking simultaneously with our reading or hearing it. Parts of the novel suggest that the act of storytelling is more important than any ethical concerns of the particular story told; other aspects of the novel elevate that idea to confirm that stories themselves—the ordinary stories of ordinary people, or the stories of ordinary people made extraordinary through their stories—re-create the world.

Relatively early in the novel, Tayo's grandmother responds to his aunt's concern about gossip not with outrage but with glee, for she knows worse stories about the woman gossiping about them. The novel suggests that Auntie takes some self-righteous pleasure in the possibility that her family members create opportunities for others to gossip, for she looks more respectable in comparison. Yet Tayo's grandmother barely listens to Auntie's complaints once she realizes that a story in her possession will trump anything that can be said about her family.

Later, Tayo's grandmother speaks the last word before the novel concludes with two ceremonial poems. After listening to the story of Pinkie's death at Emo's hands, the grandmother sighs, almost with boredom, for there's nothing new in this story: "It seems like I already heard these stories before...only thing is, the names sound different" (260). This story, in other words, has been enacted for eons—it's a story of witchery and ceremony, evil and good. During this particular enactment, Pinkie and Emo have assumed roles that had been taken on by others in the past. Because Pinkie and Emo willingly participated with the destroyers, because they have assumed the identity of destroyers, they suffer from their own style of destruction. Because Tayo's grandmother has heard this story so many times already, she knows how it will end, with the destroyers being destroyed.

Yet for the ceremony that is the novel to be effective, the story must be told properly. When Ku'oosh begins the scalp ceremony, he instructs Tayo that "this world is fragile" (35). The narrator explains the connotations of the word Ku'oosh had used to express the concept of "fragile," and Ku'oosh's explanation continues intricately, with each word explained through its connotations. Each word is accompanied by its own story. Because a word's connotations are so important, a story can be told with particular words only, not simply because language conveys meaning but because words create the world. In order for the world to continue, the correct words must be spoken. Ku'oosh asserts that this manner of storytelling is "the responsibility that went with being human" (35). Although human beings affect the world in many ways, they have been given the task of maintaining the world through their use of language.

With Tayo's grandmother's last words, her memories of hearing these stories before, the novel is complete—except for the ceremonial poems that follow. They suggest that the story has been properly told, that humans in the book have accepted their responsibility. Witchery has not conquered the world, the poem assures the reader. The novel ends nearly as it begins, with a chant to the sunrise, with a request that the sunrise "accept this offering" (262). "This offering" is the particular chant, yet it is also the novel itself. Silko has sent an offering out into the world. By concluding with this chant to greet a new day, the narrator, Thought-Woman's creation, implies that the world will continue, that the ceremony has not simply cured Tayo but has more significantly worked to reestablish harmony within all of creation.

TOPICS FOR WRITTEN OR ORAL EXPLORATION

1. Write an analysis of one of the major characters in the novel. If the character grows or changes throughout the book, how does that change occur?

2. Make a chart placing all of the events described in the novel in chronological order. How would the effect of the novel have been different if Silko had revealed the events in this order?

3. List all of the conflicts in the novel. How are they resolved by the end? Are any left unresolved?

4. Choose one or more of the passages set as poetry and write an essay analyzing how those passages illustrate any of the themes that emerge from the prose portions of the novel.

5. Trace the imagery related to one or more particular animals throughout the novel. How are animals associated with particular characters? What do these associations reveal about the characters?

6. Imagine you are filming *Ceremony* as a movie. What would the sets look like? Which actors would you like to hire to play each character? Where would the focus of the camera be in each scene?

7. Write a story in which you place a minor character from *Ceremony* as the protagonist. Show aspects of that character's life that are not included in the novel.

8. Assume the point of view of a character other than Tayo. Describe Tayo from the perspective of that other character.

9. Read *Storyteller,* also written by Leslie Marmon Silko. At what points does it overlap with *Ceremony*? How do the two books correspond? What are the major differences between them? How does reading one help you to understand the other?

10. Compare a theme in *Ceremony* with a similar theme from another Native American novel. You might consider *House Made of Dawn* by N. Scott Momaday, *Tracks* by Louise Erdrich, *The Death of Jim Loney* by James Welch, or *Red Earth* by Philip Red Eagle.

11. Research the mythology of another Native American tribe and compare or contrast what you learn with the myths present in *Ceremony.*

12. Research the mythology of a European, Asian, or African culture. How do that culture's myths describe the relationships between human beings and other animals? How do these myths compare to those presented in *Ceremony*?

13. Write a myth of your own that accounts for the presence of people of different races. Write another myth that explains how evil came into the world.

14. Write an essay describing a ceremony you have witnessed or participated in. What effect did this ceremony have on the people present?

SUGGESTED READING

Allen, Paula Gunn. *The Sacred Hoop: Recovering the Feminine in American Indian Tra-ditions.* Boston: Beacon Press, 1986.

Arnold, Ellen L. *Conversations with Leslie Marmon Silko.* Jackson: University of Mis-sissippi Press, 2000.

Chavkin, Allan, ed. *Leslie Marmon Silko's Ceremony: A Casebook.* New York: Oxford University Press, 2002.

Erdrich, Louise. *Love Medicine.* New York: HarperPerennial, 1993.

———. *Tracks.* New York: Henry Holt and Co., 1988.

Graulich, Melody, ed. *"Yellow Woman": Leslie Marmon Silko.* New Brunswick: Rut-gers University Press, 1993.

Krupat, Arnold. *Red Matters: Native American Studies.* Philadelphia: University of Pennsylvania Press, 2002.

———. *The Turn to the Native: Studies in Criticism and Culture.* Lincoln: University of Nebraska Press, 1998.

Lincoln, Kenneth. *Native American Renaissance.* Berkeley: University of California Press, 1983.

Momaday, N. Scott. *House Made of Dawn.* New York: Harper & Row, 1968.

Owens, Louis. *Other Destinies: Understanding the American Indian Novel.* Norman: University of Oklahoma Press, 1992.

Rainwater, Catherine. *Dreams of Fiery Stars: The Transformations of Native American Fiction.* Philadelphia: University of Pennsylvania Press, 1999.

Salyer, Gregory. *Leslie Marmon Silko.* New York: Twayne, 1997.

Seyersted, Per. *Leslie Marmon Silko.* Western Writers Series 45. Boise: Boise State Uni-versity Press, 1980.

Silko, Leslie Marmon. *Almanac of the Dead.* New York: Simon & Schuster, 1991.

———. *Gardens in the Dunes.* New York: Simon & Schuster, 1999.

———. *Laguna Woman: Poems by Leslie Silko.* New York: Greenfield Review Press, 1974.

———. *Sacred Water: Narratives and Pictures.* Tucson: Flood Plain Press, 1993.

———. *Storyteller.* New York: Viking, 1981.

———. *Yellow Woman and a Beauty of the Spirit: Essays on Native American Life Today.* New York: Simon & Schuster, 1996.

Silko, Leslie Marmon, and Lee Marmon. *Rain.* New York: Whitney Museum, 1996.

Swann, Brian. *Coming to Light: Contemporary Translations of the Native Literatures of North America.* New York: Vintage, 1996.

Swann, Brian, and Arnold Krupat, eds. *Here First: Autobiographical Essays by Native American Writers.* New York: Modern Library, 2000.

Velie, Alan R. *Four American Indian Literary Masters: N. Scott Momaday, James Welch, Leslie Marmon Silko, and Gerald Vizenor.* Norman: University of Oklahoma Press, 1982.

Vizenor, Gerald, ed. *Narrative Chance: Postmodern Discourse on Native American In-dian Literatures.* Albuquerque: University of New Mexico Press, 1989.

Warrior, Robert Allen. *Tribal Secrets: Recovering American Indian Intellectual Traditions.* Minneapolis: University of Minnesota Press, 1994.

Weaver, Jace, ed. *Native American Religious Identity: Unforgotten Gods.* Maryknoll: Orbis, 1998.

————. *That the People Might Live: Native American Literatures and Native American Community.* New York: Oxford University Press, 1997.

Welch, James. *The Death of Jim Loney.* New York: Penguin, 1979.

————. *Winter in the Blood.* New York: Penguin, 1974.

Womack, Craig S. *Red on Red: Native American Literary Separatism.* Minneapolis: University of Minnesota Press, 1999.

Wright, Ann, ed. *The Delicacy and Strength of Lace: Letters Between Leslie Marmon Silko and James Wright.* St. Paul: Graywolf Press, 1986.

2

Historical Context:
Laguna Pueblo

CHRONOLOGY

10,000 B.C.	Archaeological evidence suggests that people were living throughout the Pueblo region of the current American Southwest.
1000 B.C.	Additional archaeological evidence suggests that staple crops such as corn, beans, and squash were cultivated by this point.
300 B.C.	People in the Pueblo region lived in permanent structures.
1150–1300 A.D.	Several present-day pueblos are inhabited, including Acoma, Santa Ana, and Zia.
November 1528	A Spanish shipwreck occurs near the Texas coast; eight years later, four survivors reach Mexico.
1540	Francisco Vasquez de Coronado leads his soldiers as well as civilians in an exploration of the Pueblo region.
7 July 1598	Pueblo leaders meet with Spanish representatives and declare their allegiance to the Spanish king.
1598–1680	Most prominent presence of Spanish missionaries among Pueblos.
10 August 1680	Pueblo revolt.
1680–92	Period of Pueblo independence from Spanish authority.
1693	Spanish return.
2 July 1698	Pueblo of San Jose de Laguna established.
24 August 1821	Treaty of Cordoba transfers authority over region from Spain to Mexico.

2 February 1848	Treaty of Guadalupe Hidalgo concludes war between the United States and Mexico; Pueblo region transferred to United States.
1912	New Mexico becomes a state.
1924	Indian Citizenship Act passed.
1924	Pueblo Lands Act passed.
1934	Indian Reorganization Act passed.
1948	Native Americans achieve the right to vote in New Mexico.
1949	Laguna Pueblo constitution approved.

CEREMONY AND LAGUNA PUEBLO

Much of the action of *Ceremony* occurs in or near Laguna Pueblo, about 70 miles west of Albuquerque. After a stint in the army and some time in a veterans' psychiatric facility, Tayo has returned to his original community. Several conflicts within the novel occur as a result of Tayo's ambiguous status within Laguna, since his father was white and his mother lived a disreputable life, abandoning him in the process. Although specific references to Laguna occur infrequently, the setting is crucial, in part, because the ceremony Tayo must complete in order to regain his health is directly linked to Laguna. In addition, Native American identity is often crucially associated with a person's relationship to land in general and to a particular place. Tayo is not simply from Laguna; he is Laguna. One approach to analyzing the plot of *Ceremony* would be to compare the type of action that occurs on Laguna and the type that occurs elsewhere.

Early in the novel, Tayo arrives at New Laguna, a town on the Laguna reservation, having traveled by train from California where he had been in the veterans' hospital. Laguna is significant here not simply as a particular pueblo but as Tayo's home. His illness has resulted not only from the war but also from aspects of his Laguna past, and his recuperation will necessarily occur in the context of that past. When the old man Ku'oosh begins to describe the ceremony, Tayo recognizes the landscape Ku'oosh refers to because Tayo had already observed it near his home, and the fact that the landscape is real to Tayo encourages him to accept the old man's instructions. The words Ku'oosh chants hence acquire more concrete meaning for Tayo—the stories not only narrate the past but also reveal meaning in the present.

When Tayo was four years old, his mother had dropped him off one night at her family's home and never returned. Although he spends the rest of his childhood and adolescence at Laguna, Tayo absorbs the understanding, especially from his aunt, that he is never entirely welcome—he's not a full-blood;

his parents don't contribute to his support or even participate in Pueblo life. His father, of course, had never belonged to the pueblo, and his mother's behavior had been so embarrassing that her neighbors had once threatened to expel her from Laguna. So while Tayo grows up among his extended family, as do many Native Americans, he's still never quite brother, never quite son. Indeed, the first time Rocky ever refers to Tayo as his brother is when they're preparing to leave the pueblo and enlist in the United States military.

Tayo and other men like him, however, remain identified by Laguna, as if place informs or even creates character. Early in Tayo's recovery when he is out walking, he is picked up by his friends Harley and Leroy, who are both drunk and are accompanied by a woman named Helen Jean, presumably a prostitute. When the narrative shifts to her point of view, the men aren't identified by name but simply as "these Laguna guys" (161). Helen Jean is wary of them, especially of Tayo because he's "too quiet" and unpredictable (161). She's less afraid of them than simply prejudiced against "these reservation guys," revealing a distinction between traditional and modernized Native Americans that virtually all the characters in the novel are aware of (161). Rocky had left in part because he valued science over what his teachers had called superstition; other characters, including Tayo's mother, leave the reservation not because they disbelieve the traditional stories but because the terms white people use to describe traditional ways make them feel ashamed. Although Helen Jean's life in Gallup has been difficult and at times humiliating, she believes that Native Americans who remain on the reservation are either unwilling to surrender their traditional lifestyle or unable to survive in a modernized setting. Characters like Helen Jean and Rocky view a mainstream American lifestyle as unequivocally more desirable than life on the reservation, even if not all aspects of "the American dream" are available to them.

Yet mainstream American life results from a history that is morally complicated at best. The most overt and ironic discussion of relations between Native Americans and other American citizens occurs as Tayo attempts to recapture Josiah's cattle. The cattle have been stolen by a rancher who has fenced in his land. Tayo successfully cuts the fence and guides the cattle through the opening before he is caught trespassing by two men identified as a Texan and a cowboy. Just before they let Tayo go, the Texan says, "These goddamn Indians got to learn whose property this is!" (202). Tayo believes that the white people who have fenced in the land are themselves the thieves, that their "property" has been dishonestly acquired, and that they are destroying the world and themselves along with it. White people are haunted by their consciences, by the immoral acts of their ancestors, Tayo believes: "It was the white people who had nothing; it was the white people who were suffering as thieves do, never able to forget that their pride was wrapped in something stolen, something that had never been, and could never be, theirs" (204). This statement implies that white people need a curing ceremony as much as Tayo does. To Tayo, the boundaries that separate Laguna from the rest of New Mexico may be legal, but they are not real. The land of the American Southwest was created for certain groups of people—just as the lands of Europe and Africa and Asia were created for other groups of people—and those people remain eternally responsible for performing the ceremonies that maintain creation. According to Pueblo cosmology, the past and the present are not distinct moments of time—the present fulfills and repeats the past—so some historical events do not necessarily attain the same authority they might in another culture. The Texan's authority over the land, in other words, is unreal—an illusion because his purchase of that land was, in a cosmic sense, invalid. Tayo's vision of himself as part of a continuous landscape, and as participating in a continuous moment, is real.

EARLY PUEBLO HISTORY

Laguna Pueblo (officially San Jose de Laguna, or St. Joseph of the Lake) is one of approximately two dozen pueblos located in New Mexico and Arizona. Despite the geographic proximity and similar lifestyle of these pueblos, however, scholars believe that the Pueblo people do not all share the same ancestry. The languages spoken at the pueblos are dramatically different and generally not mutually comprehensible—a person residing at Laguna and speaking Keres, for example, would not be able to understand the Tiwa language spoken at Isleta, about 50 miles away. The ancestors of some of today's Pueblo people probably began to arrive in the region as early as 12,000 years ago; over time, these migrating ancestors likely consisted of groups from at least three different locations. One of the most prominent ancestral cultures of today's Pueblos was the Anasazi, whose influence reached its height during the twelfth century A.D. The Anasazi flourished throughout the "four corners" region of what is now the United States—the area where Utah, Colorado, New Mexico, and Arizona intersect. Since contact with Europeans began nearly 500 years ago, the various Pueblos have shared a substantial portion of their history, in part because several Pueblos formed alliances to oppose the Europeans.

The first Europeans to spend extended time in what is now New Mexico and Arizona were Spanish explorers, soldiers, and missionaries, the most famous of whom was Francisco Vasquez de Coronado. The earliest of these men had heard rumors about vast wealth to be discovered in the mythic Seven Cities of Cibola and had hoped to acquire that wealth for themselves. Of course, the rumors were exaggerated, but the soldiers persisted in their hunt, encountering several pueblos as they traveled north from Mexico. Eventually, Franciscan priests established

Catholic missions at each of these pueblos, forbidding the people to practice their traditional religions and encouraging them instead to be baptized Catholic and participate in Catholic rituals. Simultaneously, the Inquisition had reached its height in Europe, and priests often suspected the Native Americans of performing witchcraft, punishing them accordingly. Typical of European practice at this time, these punishments often consisted of appalling torture and a level of violence that most twenty-first-century readers would find horrifying: chopping off the suspects' hands or feet, for example, or burning them alive.

Tension between the Spaniards and the Native Americans arose over these sometimes forced conversions but also because the soldiers and priests demanded support from the Pueblos in the form of food and clothing. These demands grew so burdensome that some Pueblo families were driven to near starvation. Compounding the problem of this excessive tax, some Pueblo men were forced to work at maintaining the church buildings, and thus could not contribute to the agricultural work. The Pueblo people were effectively enslaved to the Spanish. Several comparatively small Pueblo groups intermittently resisted Spanish demands, attempting to force them to flee the area, but those attacks had little effect until 1680. During August of that year, the Pueblos united in a further effort to expel the Spanish; that event has come to be known as the Pueblo Revolt, during which over 400 Spaniards were killed. As a result, the Catholic missions were abandoned, and the remaining Spanish representatives fled. They stayed away for 12 years.

Unfortunately, the Pueblo enemies also included Navajo and Apache tribes, who began to raid the towns once the Spanish had abandoned them. At the invitation of some members of the Pueblos, the Spanish returned, in part to protect the Pueblos, although relations between the two groups never became unequivocally cooperative. Raids continued, and skirmishes occurred at several locations over the next century.

PUEBLO HISTORY UNDER MEXICO AND THE UNITED STATES

In 1821, Mexico—including much territory currently considered part of the American Southwest—became independent of Spain. In an unusual declaration, Mexico stated that all residents regardless of ethnicity would share equal citizenship. Most radically, Mexico did not consider Native Americans as separate from the rest of its society, as the United States generally did. Although such an understanding did not significantly alter daily life on the pueblos, which were far from the Mexican capital, the question of citizenship would profoundly affect the relationship of Pueblos with the United States.

Although this region would remain under Mexican rule for about 25 years, changes were also occurring in the United States that would influence how the Pueblos would be received by the United States. Most notably, the Bureau of Indian Affairs (BIA) was created as a division of the Department of War. Obviously, the government of the United States perceived its relations with any and all Native American tribes as primarily military and presumably hostile—otherwise the BIA could have been housed in a different department. (The BIA eventually was transferred to the Department of the Interior.) Then in 1834 Congress passed the Indian Trade and Intercourse Act, which made it a federal crime for a non–Native American to settle on Native American land. On the one hand, this law protected reservations from encroachment by American settlers whose increasing presence threatened to eradicate traditional native life. Yet it also precluded the tribes from exercising complete authority over their own land if, for example, they believed they would be better served to permit white settlers on their land.

In 1846 the United States entered a controversial war against Mexico. When the war was concluded with the signing of the Treaty of Guadalupe Hidalgo in 1848, the United States acquired thousands of square miles of land from Mexico, including what is now New Mexico and Arizona. Pueblo Native Americans were now residents of the United States, but their status as citizens would become confused. Ostensibly, the Treaty of Guadalupe Hidalgo transferred their rights as citizens, yet the United States was not accustomed to treating Native Americans as citizens. Some Americans argued that because the Pueblos lived in permanent towns supported through agriculture rather than living as nomadic tribes more often supported through hunting, the Pueblo people weren't "really" Native Americans—and the laws that had been passed by the United States protecting Native Americans did not apply to the Pueblos. No one, however, seriously argued that Pueblo people were identical to white people, or even had equivalent rights as white people. This debate points to the overdetermined nature of identity and the difficulty of clearly defining ethnicity.

Because its populations remained relatively low, New Mexico remained a territory until 1912, when it was admitted to the union as a state. Twelve years later, Congress passed the Indian Citizenship Act, which declared that all Native Americans were also citizens of the United States. Not all of the privileges we normally associate with citizenship were immediately granted to Native Americans, however. New Mexico and Arizona, for example, refused to grant Native Americans the right to vote until 1948, and then only as a result of a lawsuit. Currently, all Native Americans born in the United States, whether or not they are born on a reservation, are citizens of the United States, equally with all other citizens. They may also, if they wish, be enrolled as members of particular tribes that govern themselves analogously to separate nations.

LIFE ON A PUEBLO

The word "pueblo" is Spanish for town, and the various pueblos are built as complete towns. Today, the Laguna reservation consists of several villages, including Old Laguna, Paguate, Mesita, Seama, Encinal, and Paraje. Buildings are typically erected as long apartment-style units, often about three stories high. They are constructed from adobe, a mixture of clay and sand, or mud plaster over stone. Each apartment is entered through the roof; ladders are propped against the outside of the buildings, and they can be pulled inside when the residents want to prevent others from entering. This design historically functioned as a defensive measure—enemies could not enter the buildings if the ladders were inside. During the past few centuries, pueblo architecture has been influenced by Spanish and Anglo-American styles. More recently, some modern-style housing has been built; mobile homes provide an economical alternative for several families on Laguna.

For most of their history, Pueblo people subsisted primarily on three main crops: corn, squash, and beans. They raised several varieties of each and aimed to keep at least a year's supply dried and stored in their homes because of frequent droughts that would otherwise lead to famine. Wild plants such as onions, cactus, dandelions, and various berries sometimes supplemented these staple foods. The Pueblo people also gathered nuts and wild herbs to use as flavoring. They seldom ate meat, although they occasionally hunted rabbit, deer, and antelope; the hides of these animals were sewn into clothing and the bones carved into tools. To compensate for the lack of rain, men residing at pueblos far from a river generally dug irrigation ditches. All of the major agricultural activities—opening the irrigation ditches, planting, harvesting—would be accompanied by ceremonies linking physical survival with spiritual consciousness.

Tasks assigned to a person depended on that person's gender and, to some extent, clan. Men cleared the irrigation ditches, planted the crops, gathered the harvest, and cared for any livestock. Until about three generations ago, most farming implements were wooden hand tools. Women assumed responsibility for the food after it had been harvested, grinding the corn into flour and preparing the meals. Women also performed much of the craftwork, making pottery and weaving baskets.

Although infants were generally confined to cradle boards for the first several months of their lives, parents indulged their children until they were old enough to walk. Then discipline became more important. Young children were asked to gather wood, while older children were expected to assist with more difficult tasks. If children misbehaved, their punishments most often consisted of lectures about why their actions were wrong; only in the most extreme cases would they receive physical punishment. Occasionally, other villagers masqueraded as terrifying creatures and visited children who were known to be troublesome; the masked adults would threaten to carry the children away if their behavior didn't improve.

The clan system can seem complicated since clans do not correspond exactly to other types of family structures. Anthropologists have documented between 13 and 20 different clans at Laguna Pueblo; many of these clans take their names from animals, such as the bear, lizard, eagle, and badger, but others are named for water, sun, and corn. Clan membership is matrilineal, although the father's clan is also important. Each clan has special responsibilities within the pueblo, often related to specific ceremonies. Marriage into one's own clan was traditionally strongly discouraged, and neither a man nor a woman could change clan membership at marriage. Today, however, many Native Americans marry completely outside of their tribes, choosing spouses from another race or tribal affiliation.

LAGUNA PUEBLO

In 1698 internal disagreements on several pueblos led a group of people to establish a new town, Laguna, which would become the home of Leslie Marmon Silko and a primary setting of *Ceremony.* (Different versions of the story of the establishment of Laguna Pueblo exist; at this point, it's impossible to verify any one version as absolutely correct.) Although archaeological evidence suggests that some people lived in the area well before the end of the seventeenth century, Laguna is quite young compared to other pueblos. A Christian church appears as a dominant architectural feature of each of the larger villages on the reservation; within the villages, a traditional ceremonial plaza also occupies a prominent position, although the plaza is generally much less visible to casual visitors or to travelers passing near a village on the highway.

Its history is also unusual in that white men, including Silko's great-grandfather, became politically powerful on the reservation after marrying Laguna women. Walter Marmon and his brother Robert Marmon, Silko's great-grandfather, both eventually became governor of Laguna. Their knowledge of governing systems in the United States and assumptions about the value of democracy compared to traditional tribal methods of decision making would eventually influence the governing structure of Laguna and other pueblos. Historians also believe that the Marmons persuaded the Atlantic and Pacific railroad to construct its cross-country route near Laguna at the end of the nineteenth century. The railroad increased the pace of change on the pueblo, since contact with outsiders became much more frequent. For better or worse, tourists brought new ideas, while merchants provided new goods and also introduced a cash economy that gradually replaced the barter system. Simulta-

"Laguna Pueblo, New Mexico" from *The Great Southwest,* 1914. (Courtesy Museum of New Mexico, negative number 149714)

neously, because residents of the pueblos could now reach nearby cities in hours rather than days, they began to travel off the reservation more frequently.

Today, about 7,700 people actually live on Laguna. Many members of the pueblo live off the reservation, at least for some period of time, often because employment opportunities on the reservation are scarce. Some people may commute to Albuquerque, while others live in cities farther away, such as Los Angeles or Chicago, and return to the pueblo for major ceremonies. As is true with the rest of the United States, much has changed about Laguna since the end of World War II, when *Ceremony* is set.

The following documents provide information regarding Pueblo history and life. First, an excerpt from a creation story describes the traditional understanding of how the Pueblo people arrived at their current home. Next, two documents from early exploration narratives reveal the Spanish attitudes toward the Pueblos during their initial encounters. Following those are three legal documents—a treaty and two court cases—that provide insight into the complicated relationships between the Pueblos and other governments. The final three excerpts focus on daily life within the pueblos.

TRADITIONAL CREATION STORY FROM
THE FOURTH WORLD OF THE HOPIS

   The following excerpt is a small portion of the Hopi creation narrative. The Hopis live in Arizona in pueblos quite similar to Laguna's; although they speak an Uto-Aztecan dialect rather than Keresan, and although they have had a somewhat different experience of the United States government than have the Pueblos in New Mexico, the traditional Hopi lifestyle and mythology is comparable to Laguna's. When this excerpt begins, the people have already experienced three worlds, each one situated inside the next one. They are about to climb up to the fourth, or present, world. This story includes details that address several questions that are common to creation stories: How did we get here? Why is there evil in the world? Why do people speak so many different languages? Spider Grandmother is a wisdom figure who often appears in the form of a literal spider throughout Pueblo mythology. Tawa is the sun spirit who has existed since the beginning. Although the people feel secure from evil at the end of this excerpt, they will soon discover that some evil people did climb through to the fourth world.

FROM HAROLD COURLANDER, *THE FOURTH WORLD OF THE HOPIS: THE EPIC STORY OF THE HOPI INDIANS AS PRESERVED IN THEIR LEGENDS AND TRADITIONS*

(University of New Mexico Press, 1971)

Spider Grandmother spoke... "The journey will be long and difficult. When we reach the Upper World, that will be only a beginning. Things there are not like things here. You will discover new ways of doing things. During the journey you must try to discover the meaning of life and learn to distinguish good from evil. Tawa did not intend for you to live in the midst of chaos and dissension. Only those of good heart may depart from the Third World.... As we go up the bamboo to the Upper World, see that no one carries evil medicine in his belt. See that no powakas go with us. Leave your pots and grinding stones behind.... Carry nothing that has to be held in your hands, for you will need your hands for climbing. When we have arrived in the Upper World I will tell you more about what is expected of you. Meanwhile, remember this: In the Upper World you must learn to be true humans." Then Spider Grandmother sent the people home to prepare for the journey, which would begin in four days.

As the first climbers emerged through the sipapuni and stepped into the Upper World, Yawpa the mockingbird stood at Spider Grandmother's side and sorted them out. "You shall be a Hopi and speak the Hopi language," he said to one. "You shall be a Navaho and speak the Navaho language," he said to another. "You shall be an Apache and speak the Apache language," he said to a third. He assigned every person to a tribe and a language, and to each tribe he gave a direction to go in its migrations." (24–26)

EARLY SPANISH EXPERIENCES WITH THE PUEBLOS

The next two excerpts provide an interesting contrast in terms of European interactions with Native Americans. Such narratives were generally written as official reports to the king or another superior. Some of the information in these reports is not geographically accurate due to the primitive state of maps and navigational tools of the time, but contemporary readers can often place the writers more or less accurately because of other details the writers reveal. Language barriers also often meant that the explorers or soldiers misinterpreted the acts they witnessed, occasionally humorously but sometimes disastrously. In the first excerpt, Cabeza de Vaca and his compatriots are given sustenance that literally saves their lives; in the second, Coronado's soldiers permit a number of Pueblo men to be executed unjustly. Because these two interactions occurred only a few years apart, their differences are especially startling.

Cabeza de Vaca's Experience

Cabeza de Vaca was shipwrecked off the coast of Texas in 1528. He and his fellow survivors wandered through what is now the American Southwest for approximately eight years, finally reaching Mexico with its Spanish outposts. During their journey, they suffered severe hunger and exposure to the elements. The excerpt below describes their initial meeting with Pueblo people; the town and houses the author refers to are pueblos. They are received hospitably, with the Pueblo people offering them lavish gifts, as was the Pueblo custom. The Spanish men are particularly grateful for food, and de Vaca describes how intrigued they are with the Pueblo manner of cooking. The excerpt also refers to an extended drought, demonstrating that the drought in *Ceremony* is one in a long series.

FROM *THE NARRATIVE OF ALVAR NUNEZ CABEZA DE VACA*
IN *SPANISH EXPLORERS IN THE SOUTHERN UNITED STATES,
1528–1543*, ED. FREDERICK W. HODGE

(Charles Scribner's Sons, 1907)

At the end of three days' travel we stopped, and the next day Alonzo del Castillo set out with Estevanico the negro, taking the two women as guides. She that was the captive led them to the river which ran between some ridges [the Rio Grande], where was a town at which her father lived; and these habitations were the first seen, having the appearance and structure of houses.

Here Castillo and Estevanico arrived, and, after talking with the Indians, Castillo returned at the end of three days to the spot where he had left us, and brought five or six of the people. He told us he had found fixed dwellings of civilization, that the inhabitants lived on beans and pumpkins, and that he had seen maize. This news the most of anything delighted us, and for it we gave infinite thanks to our Lord. Castillo told us the negro was coming with all the population to wait for us in the road not far off. Accordingly we left, and having travelled a league and a half, we met the negro and the people coming to receive us. They gave us beans, many pumpkins, calabashes, blankets of cowhide and other things. As this people and those who came with us were enemies, and spoke not each other's language, we discharged the latter, giving them what we received, and we departed with the others. Six leagues from there, as the night set in we arrived at the houses, where great festivities were made over us. We remained one day, and the next set out with these Indians. They took us to the settled habitations of others, who lived upon the same food.

From that place onward was another usage. Those who knew of our approach did not come out to receive us on the road as the others had done, but we found them in their houses, and they had made others for our reception. They were all seated with their faces turned to the wall, their heads down, the hair brought before their eyes, and their property placed in a heap in the middle of the house. From this place they began to give us many blankets of skin; and they had nothing they did not bestow. They have the finest persons of any people we saw, of the greatest activity and strength, who best understood us and intelligently answered our inquiries. We called them the Cow nation, because most of the cattle killed are slaughtered in their neighborhood, and along up that river for over fifty leagues they destroy great numbers.

They go entirely naked after the manner of the first we saw. The women are dressed with deer-skin, and some few men, mostly the aged, who are incapable of fighting. The country is very populous. We asked how it was they did not plant maize. They answered it was that they might not lose what they should put in the ground; that the rains had failed for two years in succession, and the seasons were so dry the seed had everywhere been taken by the moles, and they could not venture to plant again until after water had fallen copiously. They begged us to tell the sky to rain, and to pray for it, and we said we would do so. We also desired to know whence they got the maize, and they told us from where the sun goes down; there it grew throughout the region, and the nearest was by that path. Since they did not wish to go thither, we asked by what direction we might best proceed, and bade them inform us concerning the way; they said the path was along up by that river towards the north, for otherwise in a journey of seventeen days we should find nothing to eat, except a fruit they call cha-can, that is ground between stones, and even then it could with difficulty be eaten for its dryness and pungency,—which was true. They showed it to us there, and we could not eat it. They informed us also that, whilst we travelled by the river upward, we should all the way pass through a people that were their enemies, who spoke their tongue, and, though they had nothing to give us to eat, they would receive us with the best good will, and present us with mantles of cotton, hides, and other articles of their wealth. Still it appeared to them we ought by no means to take that course.

Doubting what it would be best to do, and which way we should choose for suit-ableness and support, we remained two days with these Indians, who gave us beans and pumpkins for our subsistence. Their method of cooking is so new that for its strangeness I desire to speak of it; thus it may be seen and remarked how curious and diversified are the contrivances and ingenuity of the human family. Not having discovered the use of pipkins, to boil what they would eat, they fill the half of a large calabash with water, and through [sic] on the fire many stones of such as are most convenient and readily take the heat. When hot, they are taken up with tongs of sticks and dropped into the calabash until the water in it boils from the fervor of the stones. Then whatever is to be cooked is put in, and until it is done they con-tinue taking out cooled stones and throwing in hot ones. Thus they boil their food. (102–5)

Coronado's Interactions with the Pueblo People

The next excerpt illustrates why the Pueblo people became so suspicious and resentful of Spanish intrusions. Coronado was a Spanish general who, ac-cording to many standards, successfully explored the American Southwest, al-though he never discovered the fabulous wealth that had formed part of his motive. In fact, his two-year expedition proved, to the dismay of many, that a mythically wealthy city did not exist in the area Coronado and his soldiers carefully explored. Several hundred soldiers accompanied him on this mission, and they expected support from the Native Americans they encountered. Events such as the ones described below eventually led to the successful Pueblo Revolt in 1680. First, the Pueblos are ordered to provide sufficient clothing for the Spanish, even if it means giving up their own. Then a Spanish soldier attempts to rape a Pueblo woman. He escapes punishment, and the outraged Pueblos begin killing the horses that belonged to the soldiers. Hostilities es-calate until hundreds of Pueblo people are burned at the stake. The Spanish intended, in part, to create terror among other Pueblos—any Native Ameri-can who interfered with Spanish goals would be punished this way. They suc-ceeded, but their success would eventually also cost many Spanish lives.

FROM PEDRO CASTAÑEDA, *THE JOURNEY OF CORONADO,* TRANS. GEORGE PARKER WINSHIP

(Allerton Book Co., 1922)

... [T]he general wished to obtain some clothing to divide among his soldiers, and for this purpose he summoned one of the chief Indians of Tiguex, with whom he had already had much intercourse and with whom he was on good terms, who was called Juan Aleman by our men, after a Juan gentleman who lived in Mexico, whom he was said to resemble. The general told him that he must furnish about three hundred or more pieces of cloth, which he needed to give his people. He [Juan] said that he was not able to do this, but that it pertained to the governors; and that besides this, they would have to consult together and divide it among the villages, and that it was necessary to make the demand of each town separately. The general did this, and ordered certain of the gentlemen who were with him to go and make the demand; and as there were twelve villages, some of them went on one side of the river and some on the other. As they were in very great need, they did not give the natives a chance to consult about it, but when they came to a village they demanded what they had to give, so that they could proceed at once. Thus these people could do nothing except take off their own cloaks and give them to make up the number demanded of them. And some of the soldiers who were in these parties, when the collectors gave them some blankets or cloaks which were not such as they wanted, if they saw any Indian with a better one on, they exchanged with him without more ado, not stopping to find out the rank of the man they were stripping, which caused not a little hard feeling.

Besides what I have just said, one whom I will not name, out of regard for him, left the village where the camp was and went to another village about a league distant, and seeing a pretty woman there he called her husband down to hold his horse by the bridle while he went up; and as the village was entered by the upper story, the Indian supposed he was going to some other part of it. While he was there the Indian heard some slight noise, and then the Spaniard came down, took his horse, and went away. The Indian went up and learned that he had violated, or tried to violate, his wife, and so he came with the important men of the town to complain that a man had violated his wife, and he told how it happened. When the general made all the soldiers and the persons who were with him come together, the Indian did not recognize the man, either because he had changed his clothes for whatever other reason there may have been, but he said that he could tell the horse, because he had held his bridle, and so he was taken to the stables, and found the horse, and said that the master of the horse must be the man. He denied doing it, seeing that he had not been recognized, and it may be that the Indian was mistaken in the horse; anyway, he went off without getting any satisfaction. The next day one of the Indians, who was guarding the horses of the army, came running in, saying that a companion of his had been killed, and that the Indians of the country were driving off the horses toward their villages. The Spaniards tried to collect the horses again, but many were lost, besides seven of the general's mules.

The next day Don Garcia Lopez de Cardenas went to see the villages and talk with the natives. He found the villages closed by palisades and a great noise inside, the horses being chased as in a bull fight and shot with arrows. They were all ready for fighting. Nothing could be done, because they would not come down on to the plain and the villages are so strong that the Spaniards could not dislodge them. The general then ordered Don Garcia Lopez de Cardenas to go and surround one village with all the rest of the force. This village was the one where the greatest injury had been done and where the affair with the Indian woman occurred. Several captains who had gone on in advance with the general, Juan de Saldivar and Barrionuevo and Diego Lopez and Melgosa, took the Indians so much by surprise that they gained the upper story, with great danger, for they wounded many of our men from within the houses. Our men were on top of the houses in great danger for a day and a night and part of the next day, and they made some good shots with their crossbows and muskets. The horsemen on the plain with many of the Indian allies from New Spain smoked them out from the cellars into which they had broken, so that they begged for peace.

Pablo de Melgosa and Diego Lopez, the alderman from Seville, were left on the roof and answered the Indians with the same signs they were making for peace, which was to make a cross. They then put down their arms and received pardon. They were taken to the tent of Don Garcia, who, according to what he said, did not know about the peace and thought that they had given themselves up of their own accord because they had been conquered. As he had been ordered by the general not to take them alive, but to make an example of them so that the other natives would fear the Spaniards, he ordered 200 stakes to be prepared at once to burn them alive. Nobody told him about the peace that had been granted them, for the soldiers knew as little as he, and those who should have told him about it remained silent, not thinking that it was any of their business. Then when the enemies saw that the Spaniards were binding them and beginning to roast them, about a hundred men who were in the tent began to struggle and defend themselves with what there was there and with the stakes they could seize. Our men who were on foot attacked the tent on all sides, so that there was great confusion around it, and then the horsemen chased those who escaped. As the country was level, not a man of them remained alive, unless it was some who remained hidden in the village and escaped that night to spread throughout the country the news that the strangers did not respect the peace they had made, which afterward proved a great misfortune. After this was over, it began to snow, and they abandoned the village and returned to the camp just as the army came from Cibola. (47–52)

LEGAL DOCUMENTS AFFECTING THE PUEBLOS

The next three documents provide further insight into the conflicts between the Pueblos and civil governments created by Europeans and, eventually, Mexicans and Americans. Disagreement among Americans, particularly about how to classify the Pueblos, exacerbated these conflicts. Most often, the United States government and Americans generally believed that Native American cultures were inherently inferior to European traditions. Some Americans believed that native culture was so inferior that all Native Americans would simply die out as the boundaries of the United States progressed westward. Other Americans, the more liberal faction at that time, believed that Native Americans should be educated in European ways, forcibly if necessary. The most important habits to change included religion—several Christian denominations operated elementary schools on reservations, with the blessing of the federal government—as well as clothing, hairstyle, housing, and employment. Because the Pueblos already lived in permanent dwellings in towns with long histories, however, they confused the image Americans often had of Indians, to the point that some white people denied that Pueblos were in fact legally Native Americans. Ethnic identity at that time, as well as in our own time, was not merely a philosophical question; significant benefits and rights depended on one's ethnic or racial classification. And the authority that determined one's classification was generally the federal government.

Pueblo Rights as Defined by the Treaty of Guadalupe Hidalgo

The Treaty of Guadalupe Hidalgo ended the Mexican-American war, which had been fought primarily as a means for the United States to acquire additional territory. Much of the treaty concerns the new boundary between the two countries. Whenever jurisdiction over geographic territory changes, however, whether the change results from war, sale, or any other event, a question arises over the legal status of that territory's inhabitants. According to this treaty, all residents of the territory that had belonged to Mexico and now would belong to the United States could choose whether to remain citizens of Mexico or become citizens of the United States. When Mexico had achieved its independence from Spain, it had declared the Pueblo people to be citizens equal to any others; therefore, the Pueblo people should have been permitted full citizenship in the United States, if they so chose. The language of the treaty seems clear on that point, but subsequent events would reveal that many Americans, including some in positions of authority and influence, assumed that the treaty did not actually extend citizenship to the Pueblos.

The treaty also makes reference to "savage tribes." This term refers to tribes that were overtly hostile to the United States, tribes that attacked American settlers as they moved west and engaged in warfare with the United States military. In 1848 the term "savage tribes" did not include the Pueblos.

FROM "TREATY OF GUADALUPE HIDALGO," FEBRUARY 2, 1848, *STATS AT LARGE OF USA, 1789–1873*, VOL. 9

(Little, Brown and Co., 1862)

Article VIII

Mexicans now established in territories previously belonging to Mexico, and which remain for the future within the limits of the United States, as defined by the present treaty, shall be free to continue where they now reside, or to remove at any time to the Mexican Republic, retaining the property which they possess in the said territories, or disposing thereof, and removing the proceeds wherever they please, without their being subjected, on this account, to any contribution, tax, or charge whatever.

Those who shall prefer to remain in the said territories may either retain the title and rights of Mexican citizens, or acquire those of citizens of the United States. But they shall be under the obligation to make their election within one year from the date of the exchange of ratifications of this treaty; and those who shall remain in the said territories after the expiration of that year, without having declared their intention to retain the character of Mexicans, shall be considered to have elected to become citizens of the United States.

In the said territories, property of every kind, now belonging to Mexicans not established there, shall be inviolably respected. The present owners, the heirs of these, and all Mexicans who may hereafter acquire said property by contract, shall enjoy with respect to it guarantees equally ample as if the same belonged to citizens of the United States.

Article IX

The Mexicans who, in the territories aforesaid, shall not preserve the character of citizens of the Mexican Republic, conformably with what is stipulated in the preceding article, shall be incorporated into the Union of the United States and be admitted at the proper time (to be judged of by the Congress of the United States) to the enjoyment of all the rights of citizens of the United States, according to the principles of the Constitution; and in the mean time, shall be maintained and protected in the free enjoyment of their liberty and property, and secured in the free exercise of their religion without restriction.

Article XI

Considering that a great part of the territories, which, by the present treaty, are to be comprehended for the future within the limits of the United States, is now occupied by savage tribes, who will hereafter be under the exclusive control of the Government of the United States, and whose incursions within the territory of Mexico would be prejudicial in the extreme, it is solemnly agreed that all such incursions shall be forcibly restrained by the Government of the United States whensoever this may be necessary; and that when they cannot be prevented, they shall be punished by the said Government, and satisfaction for the same shall be exacted all in the same way, and with equal diligence and energy, as if the same incursions were meditated or committed within its own territory, against its own citizens.

It shall not be lawful, under any pretext whatever, for any inhabitant of the United States to purchase or acquire any Mexican, or any foreigner residing in Mexico, who may have been captured by Indians inhabiting the territory of either of the two republics; nor to purchase or acquire horses, mules, cattle, or property of any kind, stolen within Mexican territory by such Indians.

And in the event of any person or persons, captured within Mexican territory by Indians, being carried into the territory of the United States, the Government of the latter engages and binds itself, in the most solemn manner, so soon as it shall know of such captives being within its territory, and shall be able so to do, through the faithful exercise of its influence and power, to rescue them and return them to their country, or deliver them to the agent or representative of the Mexican Government. The Mexican authorities will, as far as practicable, give to the Government of the United States notice of such captures; and its agents shall pay the expenses incurred in the maintenance and transmission of the rescued captives; who, in the mean time, shall be treated with the utmost hospitality by the American authorities at the place where they may be. But if the Government of the United States, before receiving such notice from Mexico, should obtain intelligence, through any other channel, of the existence of Mexican captives within its territory, it will proceed forthwith to effect their release and delivery to the Mexican agent, as above stipulated.

For the purpose of giving to these stipulations the fullest possible efficacy, thereby affording the security and redress demanded by their true spirit and intent, the Government of the United States will now and hereafter pass, without unnecessary delay, and always vigilantly enforce, such laws as the nature of the subject may require. And, finally, the sacredness of this obligation shall never be lost sight of by the said Government, when providing for the removal of the Indians from any portion of the said territories, or for its being settled by citizens of the United States; but, on the contrary, special care shall be taken not to place its Indian occupants under the necessity of seeking new homes, by committing those invasions which the United States have solemnly obliged themselves to restrain.

Pueblo Status According to *United States v. Joseph*

On June 30, 1834—when Pueblo territory fell within Mexico—the Congress of the United States passed a law called the Indian Trade and Intercourse Act. This act made it illegal for any non-Indian to settle on Indian territory, much of which was by this time regulated according to the reservation system. That is, the United States government considered the land ultimately to belong to the United States, but it was "reserved" for particular tribal use. As a result of this law, none of this land could be sold outside the tribe, since the tribe held the land for the use of its members but didn't actually own it.

In *United States v. Joseph,* the Supreme Court ruled that because the land occupied by Taos Pueblo was in fact owned by them, that their ownership of that land was declared in the Treaty of Guadalupe Hidalgo, the Pueblos were not covered by the 1834 Indian Trade and Intercourse Act. Subsequently, approximately 3,000 white families settled on Pueblo land, significantly diminishing the Pueblos' ability to support themselves.

In the excerpt below, the Court asks whether Pueblos are "Indians," "within the meaning of the statute." That is, did this particular law intend to include Pueblos? The Court is not suggesting that the Pueblos are anything but Native American ethnically. In fact, the Court quotes the chief justice of the lower court who had stated that the Pueblos were Native American in their appearance, but in few other ways. That judge suggested that the definition of "Indian" also included such things as lifestyle, education—or the lack of it, and intelligence—or the lack of it, a suggestion the Supreme Court seems to accept. Interestingly, in this case, the descriptions of the Pueblos are consistently positive, at least compared to other tribes.

FROM *UNITED STATES V. JOSEPH,* 94 U.S. 614, 4 OTTO 614, 24 L. ED. 295 (1876)

The case before us was an action brought by the United States in the proper court in the Territory of New Mexico.... The petition alleges that defendant "did make a settlement in, and now occupies and is settled on, lands of the pueblo tribe of Indians of the pueblo of Taos, in the county of Taos, to wit, ten acres of land (describing its boundaries), by then and there building houses and making fields thereon.... Said lands then and there, and at the time of bringing this suit, belonging to said pueblo tribe of Indians of the pueblo of Taos aforesaid, and secured to said pueblo tribe of Indians of the pueblo of Taos aforesaid, by patent from the United States."

A demurrer to this petition was sustained in the Supreme Court of the Territory, and we are called on to decide whether it was rightfully sustained.

Were the pueblo Indians, and the lands held by them, on which this settlement was made, within the meaning of the act of Congress of 1834, and its extension to the Territory of New Mexico, by the act of 1851? This question resolves itself into two other:—

1. Are the people who constitute the pueblo or village of Taos an Indian tribe within the meaning of the statute?

2. Do they hold the lands on which the settlement mentioned in the petition was made by a tenure which brings them within its terms?

The first question is not concluded even on demurrer, because the petition calls them "the pueblo tribe of Indians of the pueblo of Taos;" for if these people, with others of the same character, are a well-known class, whose history, domestic habits, and relations to the government are matters of public notoriety, the court, being informed who they are by the description of them in the petition, as "pueblo Indians of the Pueblo of Taos," is not bound by the use of the additional word "tribe" to disregard that knowledge, and assume that they are tribal Indians within the meaning of the statute regulating the intercourse of the white man with this latter class of Indians.

The character and history of these people are not obscure, but occupy a well-known page in the story of Mexico, from the conquest of the country by Cortez to the cession of this part of it to the United States by the treaty of Guadaloupe Hidalgo. The subject is tempting and full of interest, but we have only space for a few well-considered sentences of the opinion of the chief justice of the court whose judgment we are reviewing.

"For centuries," he says, "the pueblo Indians have lived in villages, in fixed communities, each having its own municipal or local government. As far as their history can be traced, they have been a pastoral and agricultural people, raising flocks and cultivating the soil. Since the introduction of the Spanish Catholic missionary into the country, they have adopted mainly not only the Spanish language, but the religion of a Christian church. In every pueblo is erected a church, dedicated to the worship of God, according to the form of the Roman Catholic religion, and in nearly all is to be found a priest of this church, who is recognized as their spiritual guide and adviser. They manufacture nearly all of their blankets, clothing, agricultural and culinary implements, &c. Integrity and virtue among them is fostered and encouraged. They are as intelligent as most nations or people deprived of means or facilities for education. Their names, their customs, their habits, are similar to those of the people in whose midst they reside, or in the midst of whom their pueblos are situated. The criminal records of the courts of the Territory scarcely contain the name of a pueblo Indian. In short, they are a peaceable, industrious, intelligent, honest, and virtuous people. They are Indians only in feature, complexion, and a few of their habits; in all other respects superior to all but a few of the civilized Indian tribes of the country, and the equal of the most civilized thereof. This description of the pueblo Indians, I think, will be deemed by all who know them as faithful and true in all respects. Such was their character at the time of the acquisition of New Mexico by the United States; such is their character now."

At the time the act of 1834 was passed there were no such Indians as these in the United States, unless it be one or two reservations or tribes, such as the Senecas or Oneidas of New York, to whom, it is clear, the eleventh section of the statute could have no application. When it became necessary to extend the laws regulating intercourse with the Indians over our new acquisitions from Mexico, there was ample room for the exercise of those laws among the nomadic Apaches, Comanches, Navajoes [*sic*], and other tribes whose incapacity for self-government required both for themselves and for the citizens of the country this guardian care of the general government.

The pueblo Indians, if, indeed, they can be called Indians, had nothing in common with this class. The degree of civilization which they had attained centuries before, their willing submission to all the laws of the Mexican government, the full recognition by that government of all their civil rights, including that of voting and holding office, and their absorption into the general mass of the population (except that they held their lands in common), all forbid the idea that they should be classed with the Indian tribes for whom the intercourse acts were made, or that in the intent of the act of 1851 its provisions were applicable to them. The tribes for whom the act of 1834 was made were those semi-independent tribes whom our government has always recognized as exempt from our laws, whether within or without the limits of an organized State or Territory, and, in regard to their domestic government, left to their own rules and traditions; in whom we have recognized the capacity to make treaties, and with whom the governments, state and national, deal, with a few exceptions only, in their national or tribal character, and not as individuals.

If the pueblo Indians differ from the other inhabitants of New Mexico in holding lands in common, and in a certain patriarchal form of domestic life, they only resemble in this regard the Shakers and other communistic societies in this country, and cannot for that reason be classed with the Indian tribes of whom we have been speaking.

We have been urged by counsel, in view of these considerations, to declare that they are citizens of the United States and of New Mexico. But abiding by the rule which we think ought always to govern this court, to decide nothing beyond what is necessary to the judgment we are to render, we leave that question until it shall be made in some case where the rights of citizenship are necessarily involved. But we have no hesitation in saying that their status is not, in the face of the facts we have stated, to be determined solely by the circumstance that some officer of the government has appointed for them an agent, even if we could take judicial notice of the existence of that fact, suggested to us in argument.

Turning our attention to the tenure by which these communities hold the land on which the settlement of defendant was made, we find that it is wholly different from that of the Indian tribes to whom the act of Congress applies. The United States have not recognized in these latter any other than a passing title with right of use, until by treaty or otherwise that right is extinguished. And the ultimate title has been always held to be in the United States, with no right in the Indians to transfer it, or even their possession, without consent of the government.

It is this fixed claim of dominion which lies at the foundation of the act forbidding the white man to make a settlement on the lands occupied by an Indian tribe.

The pueblo Indians, on the contrary, hold their lands by a right superior to that of the United States. Their title dates back to grants made by the government of Spain before the Mexican revolution,—a title which was fully recognized by the Mexican government, and protected by it in the treaty of Guadaloupe Hidalgo, by which this country and the allegiance of its inhabitants were transferred to the United States.

With the purpose of carrying into effect this provision of that treaty, Congress directed the surveyor-general of New Mexico to make inquiry into all grants of the Spanish and Mexican governments, and to report to that body on their validity. Such reports were made from time to time, one of which included, and recommended for confirmation, this claim of "the pueblo of Taos, in the county of Taos," not the pueblo Indians of Taos, but the pueblo of Taos; and by an act of Congress of Dec. 22, 1858, 11 Stat. 374, the title was confirmed, and the commissioner of the land-office ordered to "issue the necessary instructions for the survey of all of said claims, as recommended for confirmation by the said surveyor-general, and cause a patent to issue therefor [*sic*], as in ordinary cases to private individuals: Provided, that the confirmation shall only be construed as relinquishment of all title and claim of the United States to any of said lands, and shall not affect any adverse valid rights, should such exist."

It is unnecessary to waste words to prove that this was a recognition of the title previously held by these people, and a disclaimer by the government of any right of present or future interference, except such as would be exercised in the case of a person holding a competent and perfect title in his individual right.

If the defendant is on the lands of the pueblo, without the consent of the inhabitants, he may be ejected, or punished civilly by a suit for trespass, according to the laws regulating such matters in the Territory. If he is there with their consent or license, we know of no injury which the United States suffers by his presence, nor any statute which he violates in that regard.

Judgment affirmed.

Pueblo Status According to *United States v. Sandivol*

Less than forty years after *United States v. Joseph*, the Supreme Court reached an opposite conclusion in *United States v. Sandivol*. Here, the Court rejects the precedent set by *United States v. Joseph* by suggesting that the two cases are dissimilar because the Joseph case asked a much more limited type of question. The Sandivol case questions whether Congress has the authority to prohibit the sale of alcohol to the Pueblos, and the Court sees itself as ruling not simply on a matter concerning the Pueblos but on the extent of the authority of Congress. Neither case leads to a conclusion that the Pueblos are in fact citizens of the United States, despite the implications of the Treaty of Guadalupe Hidalgo; in fact, *United States v. Sandivol* especially implies that they are not. The Court seems to accept the argument that if the Pueblos are treated as citizens, that is, given authority over their own lives, they will prove themselves unable to exercise this responsibility and end up as paupers looking to the government for support. In this case, the Supreme Court concludes that the Pueblos are a primitive people, unable to function as proper citizens. The Court quotes the opinions of superintendents, presumably white men employed by the BIA, who speak of the Pueblos in much more disparaging terms than does the quotation offered in *United States v. Joseph*.

FROM *UNITED STATES V. SANDIVOL,* 231 U.S. 28, 34 S. CT. I, 58 L. ED. 107 (1913)

The question to be considered, then, is whether the status of the Pueblo Indians and their lands is such that Congress competently can prohibit the introduction of intoxicating liquor into those lands notwithstanding the admission of New Mexico into statehood.

There are as many as twenty Indian pueblos scattered over the state, having an aggregate population of over 8,000. The lands belonging to the several pueblos vary in quantity, but usually embrace about 17,000 acres, held in communal, fee-simple ownership under grants from the King of Spain, made during the Spanish sovereignty, and confirmed by Congress since the acquisition of that territory by the United States....As respects six of the pueblos, one being the Santa Clara, adjacent public lands have been reserved by Executive orders for the use and occupancy of the Indians.

The local estimate of this people is reflected by a New Mexico statute adopted in 1854, and carried into subsequent compilations, whereby there were "excluded from the privilege of voting at the popular elections of the territory" other than the election of overseers of ditches in which they were interested, and the election of the officers of their pueblos "according to their ancient customs."...

With one accord the reports of the superintendents charged with guarding their interests show that they are dependent upon the fostering care and protection of the government, like reservation Indians in general; that, although industrially superior, they are intellectually and morally inferior to many of them; and that they are easy victims to the evils and debasing influence of intoxicants. We extract the following from published reports of the superintendents:

Albuquerque, 1904: "While a few of these Pueblo Indians are ready for citizenship and have indicated the same by their energy and willingness to accept service from the railroad companies and elsewhere, and by accepting the benefits of schools and churches, a large percent of them are unable, and not yet enough advanced along the lines of civilization, to take upon themselves the burden of citizenship. It is my opinion that in the event taxation is imposed, it will be but a short time before the masses of the New Mexico Pueblo Indians will become paupers. Their lands will be sold for taxes, the whites and Mexicans will have possession of their ancient grants, and the government will be compelled to support them or witness their extermination."

Santa Fe, 1905: "Until the old customs and Indian practices are broken among this people we cannot hope for a great amount of progress. The secret dance, from which all whites are excluded, is perhaps one of the greatest evils. What goes on at this time I will not attempt to say, but I firmly believe that it is little less than a ribald system of debauchery. The Catholic clergy is unable to put a stop to this evil, and know as little of same as others. The United States mails are not permitted to pass through the streets of the pueblos when one of these dances is in session; travelers are met on the outskirts

of the pueblo and escorted at a safe distance around. The time must come when the
Pueblos must give up these old pagan customs and become citizens in fact."

During the Spanish dominion the Indians of the pueblos were treated as wards re-
quiring special protection, were subjected to restraints and official supervision in the
alienation of their property, and were the beneficiaries of a law declaring "that in the
places and pueblos of the Indians no wine shall enter, nor shall it be sold to them.". . .

But it is not necessary to dwell specially upon the legal status of this people under
either Spanish or Mexican rule, for whether Indian communities within the limits of
the United States may be subjected to its guardianship and protection as dependent
wards turns upon other considerations . . . Not only does the Constitution expressly
authorize Congress to regulate commerce with the Indian tribes, but long continued
legislative and executive usage and an unbroken current of judicial decisions have attributed to the United States as a superior and civilized nation the power and the duty
of exercising a fostering care and protection over all dependent Indian communities
within its borders, whether within its original territory or territory subsequently acquired, and within or without the limits of a state. . . .

As before indicated, by an [*sic*] uniform course of action beginning as early as 1854
and continued up to the present time, the legislative and executive branches of the
government have regarded and treated the Pueblos of New Mexico as dependent communities entitled to its aid and protection, like other Indian tribes, and, considering
their Indian lineage, isolated and communal life, primitive customs and limited civilization, this assertion of guardianship over them cannot be said to be arbitrary, but
must be regarded as both authorized and controlling. . . .

It is said that such legislation cannot be made to embrace the Pueblos, because they
are citizens. As before stated, whether they are citizens is an open question, and we
need not determine it now, because citizenship is not in itself an obstacle to the exercise by Congress of its power to enact laws for the benefit and protection of tribal Indians as a dependent people. . . .

. . . Considering the reasons which underlie the authority of Congress to prohibit
the introduction of liquor into the Indian country at all, it seems plain that this authority is sufficiently comprehensive to enable Congress to apply the prohibition to
the lands of the Pueblos.

We are not unmindful that in *United States v. Joseph* . . . there are some observations
not in accord with what is here said of these Indians, but as that case did not turn
upon the power of Congress over them or their property, but upon the interpretation
and purpose of a statute not nearly so comprehensive as the legislation now before us,
and as the observations there made respecting the Pueblos were evidently based upon
statements in the opinion of the territorial court, then under review, which are at vari-
ance with other recognized sources of information, now available, and with the long-
continued action of the legislative and executive departments, that case cannot be

regarded as holding that these Indians or their lands are beyond the range of con
gressional power under the Constitution.

Being a legitimate exercise of that power, the legislation in question does not en-
croach upon the police power of the state, or disturb the principle of equality among
the states.

DAILY LIFE ON THE PUEBLOS

The final three excerpts describe how Pueblo people lived their daily lives, specifically how they provided food for themselves and how they manufactured clay pots. The Pueblos engaged in many other crafts, too, weaving and basket making, for example. In those crafts also, the patterns and styles would vary from one pueblo to another. Despite the European influence of the last several centuries, many traditional beliefs and practices remain. Over the last 30 or 40 years, some of these beliefs have become more rather than less popular.

The Importance of Corn

Corn is a particularly popular American crop, largely because of its historic importance to Native Americans; in contrast, many Europeans use corn only as feed for animals and stare in amazement at Americans who relish corn on the cob as a special summertime treat. The following excerpt explains not only the practical significance of corn in Pueblo life, but also its spiritual significance. Because corn was so crucial to the physical survival of the people, many ceremonies, including some that occur in *Ceremony,* featured cornmeal in recognition of that fact; other ceremonies were designed specifically for the planting of corn. If the corn crop failed for more than two consecutive years, the Pueblo people would experience famine.

Converting raw corn into cornmeal, however, was a particularly arduous task, and women generally spent several hours each day grinding corn. By approaching the task communally and even ceremonially, they were able to ease some of the tedium. Just as a man was expected to be a skilled farmer if he expected to marry, a young woman was expected to demonstrate her stamina preparing the dried corn for her family's consumption.

FROM RUTH UNDERHILL, *WORK A DAY LIFE OF THE PUEBLOS* (DEPT. OF THE INTERIOR, UNITED STATES INDIAN SERVICE, 1946)

The main food of the pueblos was Indian corn.... They were grateful to this permanent crop, which had allowed them to settle down among their fields, instead of wandering with the seasons. Zuni thought of it as the flesh of the magical Corn Maidens. The Keres believed in a Corn Mother, who sent all growing things and was the mother of people also. There was hardly a ceremony in which corn, or cornmeal, was not used. Pueblo people never made animal sacrifices (indeed, few American Indians did) but when they wished to ask favors of the supernatural Beings, they scattered cornmeal.

"Grinding Corn, Pueblo Laguna, N.M." Laguna Pueblo, New Mexico. (Photo by Detroit Publishing Co., Courtesy Museum of New Mexico, negative number 40822)

...People who are not farmers may speak of corn as though it were but one kind of plant, but farmers know better. They speak of flint corn, with its hard kernels that will keep for years; flour corn, so easy to grind; dent corn, with its dimpled kernels, the prime food for cattle. Pueblo people had all of these. They began fifteen hundred years ago, with flint, in little yellow ears.... Later they had dent, half dent and flour. They did not have sweet corn and pop corn...until Whites brought it to them from other Indians.

Through the years, before this happened, they were developing the corn they did have. By 700 A.D. they had several varieties and soon they had these in different colors.... There are traditions of many-colored Indian corn from all over the country but we hear more of its importance in the pueblos than anywhere else. There were four main colors, named for the four directions from which the winds blow: yellow for north, blue for west, red for south, and white for east. Most of them also named black (really dark purple) for underground and many-colored for above. They were careful to keep the colors separate in planting but naturally there were mixtures. A bunch of pueblo corn, hanging against a wall, has as many shadings as a bouquet of flowers.

No one farmer raised all the varieties. In some towns, like Hopi, where there were at least nineteen different sorts, seeds were the property of families, carefully guarded and never given away except when a young man married and went to live with his wife's people. Then he brought with him some of his own cherished kernels for the first planting of his wife's field. We can imagine that a boy whose family owned some specially good seed, was much sought as a bridegroom.

"Ollas." Laguna Pueblo, New Mexico. (Courtesy Museum of New Mexico, negative number 23542)

All the pueblos paid special attention to their seed corn, sometimes leaving prayer feathers with it as did the Zuni, or twigs of evergreen as did the Tewa, since the never dying evergreen has a magic for growth. The dark inner rooms of pueblo houses were used for corn storage and each family often had a whole room where the ears were stacked like cord wood, each color separately. They tried to have enough for a year in advance, or even two, for there were seasons of drought when the whole crop might be lost. (30–31)

We have told of the practical side of planting. Yet the pueblo farmer felt that, in the risky task of growing food for the people, prayers and offerings were equally necessary. At Hopi and Zuni, men went racing over the plain before planting time as they hoped the torrents would race down the water courses, kicking a stick or a ball of clay before them, as the stream would roll the debris. The Tewa played shinny with a buckskin ball, full of seeds, until it burst and scattered its contents over the earth. Those villages which had irrigation ditches, opened them with prayer and ceremony, throwing feather offerings into the water. When it was time to place the seeds in the earth, there was a ritual for each individual farmer. This is the prayer of an old time Laguna man.

"Mother, Father, you who belong to the great Beings, you who belong to the Storm Clouds, you will help me. I am ready to put down yellow corn and also blue corn, and red corn and white corn and all kinds of corn. I am going to plant today. Therefore you will help me and you will make my work light. You will not make it heavy and also you will make the field not hard. You will make it soft."

Many rituals were even longer, like those described at Zuni fifty years ago.

Some morning in May the Sun Watcher would be heard calling from the house-tops that planting time had come. Then each farmer hurried to his corn room to get the special fawnskin bag in which he kept his seed corn. Zuni was one of the towns which had an especially elaborate treatment for seed corn and this had been prayed over and also sprinkled with mixture of paint, salt, flowers, and flower pollen, all holy things. The cornfield had been prayed over too. In the center the farmer had planted one of the pueblo messages to the gods, a stick decorated with the feathers of summer birds, which bring the rain. Now he took his planting stick and made six holes around the feather offering, in six directions: north, west, south, east, with northwest to represent above and southeast for below. He put four corn kernels of the appropriate color into each hole, singing:

Off yonder toward the northland (or south, east, etc.)

May it but prove that my yellow corn grains (or other color)

Shall grow and bear fruit,

Asking which I now sing.

Then he planted the rest of his corn in rows, radiating out from the center, each color by itself. This form of planting must be very old, for the Navaho learned it from the pueblos. The Hopi, however, now plant in parallel rows. They, too, make offerings, and smoke over the field. Women throw water on the men as they go out to plant, as a call to the rain to do as they are doing. Sometimes the masked figure of the god, Maa-sawu, who owns the soil, may appear by request and run around the field. (37–39)

Corn, the principal food, was not really easy to cook. There is no trouble when it is fresh, for then it can be boiled or roasted in a few minutes.... Pueblo people had to keep it for years and eat it day after day. Their corn...was usually flint corn, which has hard kernels, needing hours of cooking to soften them. Pueblo housewives had several ways of doing this. One was to grind the kernels to flour before boiling; one was to roast them until the shell cracked. One was to soak them in something like lime or lye, which would melt the shell off. Pueblo people used mostly the grinding method. They had some thirty or forty ways to cook corn and all but a few required that the sun dried kernels should first be ground into flour.

A pueblo girl, who had little to do in the way of sweeping, dishwashing or bed making, had to spend three or four hours a day grinding corn. Her flour mill consisted of three or sometimes four flat stones of different degrees of smoothness...and a small cylindrical stone which she rubbed up and down over them. When she needed flour, which was every day, she stripped the kernels from some ears of corn and laid them on the coarsest stone, then knelt behind it with the small stone in both hands and crushed them as fine as she could. The corn grew a little moist and sticky in the process, so she put it in a pot over the fire and toasted it crisp. Then she ground it on the next stone, and so on.

When she rose from the third or fourth stone her knees might be numb from kneeling. Nevertheless, every girl was expected to grind three or four quarts of meal a day, and a Hopi girl was not married until she had ground at her fiancé's house for four days to show what she could do. Three or four girls sometimes did this together, one at each stone, and the Zuni and western Keres had a ceremony in which they ground corn to music. All finished their grinding at the same time and each passed on her basket of meal to the girl at the next finer stone, with motions as rhythmical as if she were dancing. Girls do not like to grind now, say the older women, because it is so hard on their hands. At least, they are asking to use the soft flour corn and the old women do not like that. Flour corn does not resist mold and rats as the old flint use to do. (46–47)

Pueblo Pottery

Pottery making was another task assigned to women. This traditional craft was more complicated than we might initially imagine, however, for before a woman could begin designing her pot, she needed to dig the clay for herself and then create an appropriate mixture of clay and sand or some other element so that the pot would not break as it was baked. Again, spirituality was linked to practicality, and the potter would treat the earth reverently, expressing gratitude for the clay it offered. Potters are not expected to create original designs but to honor the traditions of their own villages. Therefore, a trained observer can easily recognize which pottery comes from which pueblo.

FROM RUTH UNDERHILL, *PUEBLO CRAFTS* (DEPT. OF THE INTERIOR, 1944)

Some pueblo women are still making pots. In almost every village there are a few who make plain kitchenware for their own use. With the Hopi this is quite a common thing. More often the potters make beautiful decorated ware, each in the style of her own village and sell it for ornaments....

Pueblo women have no materials ready to hand. They have to dig the clay in one place, find sand to mix with it in another, get paint in another. Each village usually has its own clay pit, or more than one, and experts can recognize pots of different pueblos by whether the clay is fine or coarse; mixed with sand or mica. In former days, each woman dug her clay with a stick and carried it home in a basket or hide. While digging, she spoke to the earth, asking permission, and perhaps leaving an offering, for pueblo people feel that clay and rocks, like animals and plants, have their own feelings, and that man must live on kindly terms with them. Today, women dig with a metal pick and carry the clay home in gunny sacks....

After the clay has been brought home, the potter has days of work ahead of her. She must pound the hard lumps fine and take out the pebbles. Then she may grind the clay on a stone, just as she grinds cornmeal, until it is soft and fine.... If she does not mean to use the clay right away, the potter wraps it in a damp cloth to keep it from hardening again. Sometimes she buries it in the ground, where it will not dry out so easily.

The next step is to mix the fine clay with some gritty material which will coarsen the texture and allow air bubbles to escape so that they do not burst or blister the pot while baking. This added grit is called temper.... Tewa women use volcanic sand which they find nearby and so do their Keresan neighbors in the Rio Grande Valley, at Domingo and Cochiti. Santa Ana and Zia pound up volcanic rock; Zuni and Acoma pound up old pottery scraps; Taos and Picuris have clay which needs no temper at all. The potter knows from experience about how much temper she will need—a fistful to a basket of clay or some such measure....

...The colors...are usually red and black. The potter pounds them to powder in a mortar, mixes them with water and keeps them in little pots sometimes four pots made all in one piece. Her brushes are sections of stiff yucca leaf, with the ends chewed into a fringe, some fine, some coarse. She places her left hand inside the pot and puts on the design with her right, perhaps measuring a little with eye and fingers to see how she is coming out. Skilled artists come out evenly, poor ones have to crowd the design but none of them sketch it in beforehand. Each potter has her characteristic patterns which, perhaps, have come down from her mother and her mother's mother. In fact, each village has its typical designs and its rules of style, and all that the individual potter does, in many cases, is to combine the traditional lines and curves in her own special way. (79–86)

One Contemporary Laguna Potter

The following excerpt describes the pottery of Gladys Paquin, who became a potter comparatively late in life. Her background includes a combination of Pueblo ancestry, and her descriptions of her pottery from a Christian perspective also demonstrate the influence of European-Native contact. Yet the pottery she molds relies on traditional Laguna designs—like Old Betonie, she adapts to contemporary culture, but she also retains traditional values. Paquin clearly understands her creativity as having a spiritual component. Yet she is also demanding of her students; only those willing to participate in the arduous task of mixing the clay can study with her.

FROM STEPHEN TRIMBLE, *TALKING WITH THE CLAY: THE ART OF PUEBLO POTTERY*

(School of American Research Press, 1987)

Pottery almost died at Laguna in the mid-twentieth century. Evelyn Cheromiah started making the old designs a few years ago, and she was joined in 1980 by Gladys Paquin.

Gladys embodies the complicated history of people and styles in today's pueblos. Born at Laguna, half Zuni, she was raised at Santa Ana. She lived in California for twenty-seven years before returning to Laguna, when, as she says, "The Lord Jesus put a desire in me to make pottery. He got me from nothing and made me a potter. Pottery is a lot like your relationship with God. God molds you and makes you and puts you in the fire."

Gladys learned the traditional ways on her own. She started with sherds as temper, but switched to volcanic ash. "The hardest part was learning how to fire, to control the fire, to know the fire. . . . Firing is so hard, but my heart tells me one of these days it will pay off."

Gladys has taken her pots to the kiln to burn off black smoke clouds from ground firing, but the kiln-fired pottery turns orange instead of red. "It looks dead, it doesn't look alive to me. The kiln sort of kills it and dries it out. When it's done outside, it looks alive. That's why I stay away from the kiln.

" . . . I ask people to collect clay and grind sherds before they come talk about how to mold. If they can't go through the whole process, they don't have it on their heart to do it. I'm not stingy with information, but unless they care they won't really work." (81–82)

TOPICS FOR WRITTEN OR ORAL EXPLORATION

1. Discuss the reasons why characters like Rocky or Helen Jean want to leave the reservation, and compare their characters to Tayo or Josiah, who seem to benefit from life at Laguna. In general, what are the advantages and disadvantages of remaining in one place for an extended period?

2. Compare the influence of the setting in *Ceremony* to other novels in which place is significant. You might consider *As I Lay Dying* by William Faulkner, *My Antonia* by Willa Cather, or *Mama Day* by Gloria Naylor.

3. The narrator states that "it was then the Laguna people understood that the land had been taken, because they couldn't stop these white people from coming to destroy the animals and the land. It was then too that the holy men at Laguna and Acoma warned the people that the balance of the world had been disturbed and the people could expect drought and harder days to come" (186). Discuss what the holy men mean by "the balance of the world."

4. Chart the major scenes of the novel. On one side of your paper list the scenes that occur at Laguna; on the other side, list the scenes that occur elsewhere. What do these lists reveal about the novel itself? about Tayo?

5. Write an essay describing the landscape of your own region or neighborhood. Research the extent to which the landscape has changed in the last 20, 30, or 100 years.

6. Research the history and contemporary presence of Native Americans in your own region or state.

7. Look up additional court cases or laws relating to Native American issues. Possibilities include *Cherokee Nation v. Georgia* (1831), *Wooster v. Georgia* (1832), The Dawes Act or General Allotment Act of 1887, *Lone Wolf v. Hitchcock* (1903), or *Quick Bear v. Leupp* (1908). Analyze the issues that initiated these court cases or led to these laws.

8. In your class, debate a current controversy involving Native Americans. Examples include repatriation of ceremonial objects, fishing rights, the use of Native American images as mascots for sports teams, and casino operation.

9. Research another moment in American history when the United States acquired additional land, the Louisiana Purchase or the purchase of Alaska, for example. What accommodations were made for native residents of those territories?

10. After reading the excerpt from *United States v. Sandivol,* discuss the stereotypes and prejudices that are evident in the court's opinion. What other stereotypes do people hold regarding Native Americans? Make a list of stereotypes that apply to other ethnic groups, such as Italian, German, Irish, Japanese, Mexican, Egyptian, and so forth.

11. Research the history of citizenship in the United States. What other groups have, at one time or another, been denied citizenship? Why? For what reasons could a person be denied citizenship today?

12. Cook a meal "from scratch"—without using any prepared foods—and then write an essay analyzing the aspects of your life that would necessarily change if you prepared all of your meals this way.

13. Write an essay describing traditional crafts of your own ethnic group. To what extent are those crafts practiced today?

SUGGESTED READING

Deloria, Vine, Jr., and David E. Wilkins. *Tribes, Treaties, and Constitutional Tribulations.* Austin: University of Texas Press, 1999.

Dozier, Edward P. *The Pueblo Indians of North America.* Prospect Heights: Waveland Press, 1983.

Eggan, Fred. *Social Organization of the Western Pueblos.* Chicago: University of Chicago Press, 1950.

Ellis, Florence Hawley. "Laguna Pueblo." *Handbook of North American Indians.* Vol. 9. Washington: The Smithsonian Institution, 1979. 438–49.

Hammond, George P., and Agapito Rey. *The Rediscovery of New Mexico, 1580–1594.* Albuquerque: University of New Mexico Press, 1966.

Knaut, Andrew L. *The Pueblo Revolt of 1680: Conquest and Resistance in Seventeenth-Century New Mexico.* Norman: University of Oklahoma Press, 1995.

Mails, Thomas E. *The Pueblo Children of the Earth Mother.* 2 vols. Garden City, NY: Doubleday, 1983.

Nabokov, P. *Native American Testimony, A Chronicle of Indian-White Relations from Prophecy to the Present.* New York: Penguin, 1991.

Parsons, Elsie Clews. *Laguna Genealogies.* New York: American Museum of Natural History, 1923.

Sando, Joe S. *Pueblo Nations: Eight Centuries of Pueblo Indian History.* Santa Fe: Clear Light Publishers, 1992.

Spicer, Edward H. *Cycles of Conquest: The Impact of Spain, Mexico, and the United States on the Indians of the Southwest, 1533–1960.* Tucson: University of Arizona Press, 1962.

Wilson, James. *The Earth Shall Weep: A History of Native America.* New York: Grove Press, 1998.

3

Historical Context: World War II and the Development of the Atomic Bomb

CHRONOLOGY

1 September 1939	Hitler's Germany attacks Poland, traditionally viewed as beginning of World War II.
3 September 1939	Great Britain and France declare war on Germany; United States declares intention to remain neutral.
4 November 1939	President Roosevelt signs Neutrality Act.
17 April 1940	United States grows suspicious about Japanese activity in the Pacific and warns Japan not to initiate aggression.
21 June 1940	France surrenders to Germany.
25 June 1940	Japan expresses intention to invade French Indochina.
20 July 1940	Roosevelt urges the United States to prepare a navy fit to fight in the Atlantic and Pacific simultaneously.
27 September 1940	Japan, Germany, and Italy sign the Tripartite Pact, creating an alliance specifically in case of war against the United States.
21 May 1941	German U-boat torpedoes American merchant ship near Brazil.
16 June 1941	United States orders German consulate offices closed and expels German diplomats.
26 July 1941	Roosevelt declares a trade embargo against Japan.
17 August 1941	Roosevelt advises Japan that United States will respond if Japan continues aggression in Pacific.

26 November 1941	Japanese naval forces begin moving toward Pearl Harbor.
7 December 1941	Japanese attack Pearl Harbor.
8 December 1941	United States declares war on Japan.
11 December 1941	Germany and Italy declare war on United States.
22 December 1941	Japanese soldiers land on Luzon in the Philippines.
23 December 1941	General MacArthur pulls American and Filipino military back into Bataan peninsula.
11 March 1942	General MacArthur leaves Philippines for Australia; will command Allied forces in southwest Pacific.
9 April 1942	Japanese capture Bataan peninsula; Bataan Death March begins.
2 December 1942	First nuclear chain reaction created at University of Chicago by Enrico Fermi.
6 June 1944	D-Day.
20 October 1944	MacArthur returns to Philippines, landing on Leyte, with intention of liberating country from Japan.
12 April 1945	Roosevelt dies; Truman becomes president of United States.
30 April 1945	Hitler commits suicide.
7 May 1945	Germany signs unconditional surrender.
8 May 1945	V-E Day.
26 June 1945	Charter of United Nations is signed by 46 countries; President Truman observes for United States but does not sign charter.
16 July 1945	First atomic bomb tested in New Mexico.
6 August 1945	United States drops atomic bomb on Hiroshima.
8 August 1945	Truman signs United Nations charter.
9 August 1945	United States drops atomic bomb on Nagasaki.
14 August 1945	Emperor Hirohito of Japan agrees to surrender.
2 September 1945	V-J Day; World War II ended.

Often when contemporary Americans discuss World War II, they focus on the events that occurred in Europe: the Battle of Normandy, the Blitz, the Holocaust. During early August we sometimes turn our attention to the anniversaries of the use of the atomic bomb, and in December we recognize the anniversary of the bombing of Pearl Harbor, but otherwise the portion of World War II set in the Pacific receives little attention. In *Ceremony*, however, Tayo serves in the Pacific, is captured by the Japanese, and survives the Bataan Death March. Back at Laguna, his grandmother notices a bright flash of light one morning, witnessing the test of the atomic bomb at Trinity, though she doesn't understand what she's seen.

WORLD WAR II AND *CEREMONY*

Soon after *Ceremony* opens, Tayo remembers a recurrent dream pattern in which he hears Japanese voices converting to Laguna voices; although the languages are not related, they share a symbolic relationship to Tayo. He is haunted by an event he was ordered to participate in during his military service. His unit had captured a number of Japanese soldiers, and the sergeant ordered the American soldiers to execute the Japanese. To Tayo, however, the Japanese soldiers remind him of his own people. The complexions and facial features of the Japanese seem similar to those of Laguna people—Asians and Native Americans resemble each other much more than either does people of European descent. Tayo sees his Uncle Josiah specifically in the man he is supposed to shoot—his Uncle Josiah who does die while he is away—and nausea incapacitates him. Despite the fact that the soldier is wearing a Japanese uniform, a fact Rocky uses to prove the soldier is not Uncle Josiah, Tayo remains convinced that Josiah has fallen and died in their midst, that American soldiers have essentially murdered his uncle.

The other Americans attribute Tayo's reaction to battle fatigue and malaria, but readers should not dismiss his response so quickly. Anthropologists believe that ancestors of the people we currently know as Native Americans did migrate from Asia, traveling across the Bering Strait, into Alaska, and then spreading south and east through what is now Canada, the United States, Mexico, and South America. (Many Native Americans reject this theory, pointing instead toward creation stories that narrate their emergence onto this continent, as the creation story excerpted in chapter 2 illustrates.) In that sense, Tayo, his uncle, and the Japanese are ancestrally related. The sergeant's order does command Tayo to execute a blood relative. One can also extrapolate from this scene to argue that all people are ancestrally related and that every person who kills another murders a relative, even in times of war or other engagements between bitter enemies. And since Uncle Josiah does die while Tayo is away, readers also need to consider the possibility that Josiah is supernaturally present among the Japanese who are executed.

Tayo had originally enlisted with the encouragement of his cousin Rocky, and they serve in the same unit in the Philippines, a unit that is captured by the Japanese and forced on what became known as the Bataan Death March. Although the recruiter had not been terribly enthusiastic about Rocky's interest in the military—he asserts that during a war, "Anyone can fight for America . . . even you boys," implying that Native Americans would be less welcome if the need were less great—Rocky nevertheless insists that he and Tayo join up. Once overseas, Rocky is seriously injured by a grenade, and Tayo and an unnamed corporal carry him on a blanket between them. Worried that the Japanese soldiers will kill Rocky if either Tayo or the corporal falls, Tayo forces himself to march through his exhaustion. When the corporal falls, a tall Japanese soldier Tayo describes as resembling a Navajo approaches them. Shoving Tayo out of the way, he "pulled the blanket over Rocky as if he were already dead, and then he jabbed the rifle butt into the muddy blanket" (44). Although the corporal attempts to persuade him that Rocky was already dead, Tayo remains haunted by the "hollow crushing sound" (44). Because of his and Rocky's roles within their family and culture, Tayo had never considered the possibility that he might survive if Rocky died.

Obviously, Tayo survives his imprisonment and eventually returns home. Like many World War II veterans, especially members of racial minorities, Tayo and his peers experience their return to civilian life as disappointing. Although they had performed heroically, at least in terms of the government's definition of heroism if not in Tayo's own mind, although they had all contributed to the American victory over the Japanese, the veterans in *Ceremony* respond to the discrimination they experience once they are out of uniform through alcohol and self-destructive violence. They convert drinking into a ritual that permits them to relive their heroism, telling war stories and joking about the sexual exploits their uniforms had permitted. For Tayo, these ritualistic escapades contribute to his continuing illness rather than assist him in readjusting to civilian life. The most violent act Tayo commits, in fact, occurs after he is home from the war and out drinking with his friends. He has recognized that the quality that made Emo a "real" soldier was his pleasure in killing, and while hearing Emo talk, Tayo discovers himself breaking his beer bottle and shoving it into Emo's belly. The violence he witnessed during the war has transformed him into a man who no longer controls his own violent impulses.

Ceremony also refers indirectly to the most violent episode of the war, the use of the atomic bomb on Hiroshima and Nagasaki. The first test of an atomic weapon occurred in New Mexico at Trinity site, southeast of Laguna. Tayo's grandmother recalls seeing a brilliant flash of light, although she is virtually blind, out her window early one morning. Her daughter doubts her story, but later that day a neighbor and the newspapers confirm it. She is puzzled about the government's motive behind such an act, and initially Tayo says he doesn't understand either. By the end of the novel, however, Tayo acknowledges that he knows the government's intentions and that the forces behind the atomic bomb are part of a universal web of evil.

WORLD WAR II IN THE PACIFIC

The United States entered World War II when Japan attacked Pearl Harbor, an American naval base in Hawaii, on December 7, 1941. For several years prior to this attack, both the United States and Japan had speculated about and prepared for a potential war in the Pacific. Japan had been preparing, in fact, to dominate the Pacific region for at least a decade before Pearl Harbor was bombed. By the time the United States entered the war, Japan already occupied much of China. The United States, however, was most concerned about the Philippines, a large group of islands still partially functioning as an American territory, although Philippine independence had been planned for. The American military expected that these islands would prove very difficult to defend for several reasons. The Philippine army itself was comparatively small, and communication was difficult because of the range of dialects spoken by Filipinos. In addition, the islands were situated only 200 miles from the closest Japanese naval base, while the American fleet was based in Hawaii, on the other side of the Pacific.

The Japanese reasoned that they would have a much better chance of winning the territory they sought—including not only the Philippines but also Burma, Malaya, Thailand, Borneo, and other islands—if they were able to destroy the American fleet before reinforcements could reach the Philippines. Therefore, they bombed Pearl Harbor, destroying 14 ships and nearly 200 aircraft. Additional Japanese victories soon followed.

During a failed attempt to defend the Philippines, General MacArthur pulled his troops onto a strip of land known as the Bataan peninsula on the island of Luzon. American and Filipino troops began to withdraw from Luzon on December 24, 1941. MacArthur initially moved to another island, Corregidor, off the tip of Luzon. Although the Japanese attacked the remaining allied troops on January 9, 1942, they did not gain a decisive victory. Under orders from President Roosevelt, MacArthur left for Australia in March. Before leaving, however, he uttered his famous vow, "I shall return." The Japanese attacked again in early April, and in order to prevent inevitable numerous casualties, Major-General Edward King surrendered his troops to the Japanese. Of the 80,000 allied troops defending the island, only about 2,000 escaped to Corregidor. The rest were captured by the Japanese and forced to walk approximately 65 miles from the town of Mariveles to San Fernando. Along the way, these soldiers were brutally treated, and many died. Those who survived the march were held in Japanese prisoner of war camps under extremely severe conditions.

After MacArthur arrived in Australia, the allies divided the Pacific into two sectors, the South-West Pacific Area commanded by MacArthur, and the Pacific Ocean Areas, commanded by Admiral Nimitz. In June 1942 the Japanese attacked Midway Island, located about 1,000 miles west of Hawaii. Because the Americans had intercepted and decoded secret Japanese communications, however, they positioned several aircraft carriers northeast of Midway and in range to defend against the Japanese attack. The strategy worked, and the American military destroyed four Japanese aircraft carriers. The battle for Guadalcanal began soon after; it would be several months before the Allies could consider themselves comfortable victors.

While these battles continued, the Allied countries debated strategy and priorities. Their combined forces were insufficient to wage full-scale battles throughout the Pacific as well as in Europe. Nevertheless, they did draft plans for American offenses, eventually hoping to retake the Philippines, an event that would presumably lead to Japanese defeat. The American advances were successful more quickly than anticipated. In October 1944 MacArthur invaded Luzon, dramatically declaring, "People of the Philippines, I have returned." Meanwhile, Admiral Nimitz's forces invaded Iwo Jima and Okinawa. Most of these battles lasted much longer than civilians, or even the soldiers, might have anticipated, due to the tenacious resistance of the Japanese military, including its use of kamikaze pilots. Most Americans assumed that an invasion of Japan itself would follow, an invasion that would likely cost thousands of lives. American scientists, however, had successfully developed the atomic bomb, and its use in August of 1945 forced Japan to surrender before an allied invasion became necessary.

THE DEVELOPMENT AND USE OF THE ATOMIC BOMB

The development of the atomic bomb depended on several scientific discoveries that had occurred during the decades preceding World War II, including several discoveries that may currently seem simple or self-evident. Radioactivity itself wasn't discovered until 1896, but almost immediately thereafter scientists speculated that the energy stored in atoms could be used for military purposes. Physicists realized that both nuclear fusion and nuclear fission could release incredible amounts of stored energy, and that this release, if a chain reaction could be created, would take the form of an explosion.

Understanding this potential event in theory was nevertheless quite different from producing an actual explosion. Some scientists believed, in fact, that the process would prove impossible, and that this impossibility was nature's way of preventing human beings from acquiring such destructive power. Such a hope, though in some ways attractive, obviously proved futile.

By 1940 scientists in several countries, including Germany and Japan as well as Great Britain and the United States, understood at least some of the theory behind nuclear reactions, although their practical capacity to create such reactions was limited. At this point, the work was pursued most urgently by the British. Although several Jewish scientists who had escaped Nazi Germany urged Albert Einstein to personally warn President Roosevelt of the potential threat of Germany's development of atomic weapons, the American government didn't feel the same degree of urgency, in part, because the United States was not yet at war.

Eventually, however, American efforts to develop atomic weapons accelerated. These efforts were consolidated under the code name of "the Manhattan Project," and laboratories were established in Los Alamos, New Mexico; Oak Ridge, Tennessee; and Hanford, Washington. Additional contributing labs, generally affiliated with universities, included those in Chicago, New York, and Berkeley, California. Scientists working on the project included Enrico Fermi, Niels Bohr, Robert Oppenheimer, and many others.

One major question scientists encountered was how to prevent the bomb from detonating until it was intended to explode. They developed two solutions, one for bombs created from uranium and one for bombs created from plutonium. Each of these solutions was tested when the United States actually did drop atomic bombs on Japan. Subsequent estimates of the cost of creating these bombs range up to $2,000,000,000, with the participation of up to 600,000 workers at various scientific and manufacturing venues around the country.

Once the bomb had been created and successfully tested, however, the major political question became not whether it could be used, but whether it should be used. If the bomb was not used, American military leaders assumed an actual invasion of Japan would be necessary to force a surrender. Because Japanese soldiers were notorious for fighting to the death rather than surrendering, such an invasion would likely cost thousands of American lives. As a means of ending the war, some scientific and political leaders argued that a demonstration of the bomb's power before international observers would be sufficient to induce Japan's surrender. (Germany had signed an unconditional surrender about one month before the bomb was tested at Trinity site during June 1945.) Others argued that only actual military use would achieve the ends the United States desired. Simultaneously, American leaders were aware that even if the war ended in an allied victory, American relations with the Soviet Union would be significantly affected by international knowledge that the United States possessed such a weapon.

After some debate, President Truman ordered the use of the atomic bomb on Japanese targets. Hiroshima was bombed on August 6, 1945, as was Nagasaki on August 9. Japan surrendered on August 10.

WORLD WAR II AND NATIVE AMERICANS

Native Americans have participated in every war the United States has fought, but the number of Native Americans fighting during World War II was particularly impressive. Over 44,000 Native American men and women joined the armed forces during the war, a figure that translates to over 10 percent of the total Native American population at that time. Although specific levels of enlistment varied from tribe to tribe, some saw up to 70 percent of their eligible men in the military. Of a total Pueblo population of 2,205, the number of men who enlisted was 213. Participating in the Philippine battles that led to the Bataan Death March were over 300 Native Americans. Native American soldiers and sailors won numerous medals, including Purple Hearts, Distinguished Flying Crosses, Bronze Stars, and Silver Stars. Three Native Americans won Congressional Medals of Honor.

Although Native Americans participated in virtually all phases of the war, their most famous contribution is probably the code developed by the Navajo Code Talkers, a code that was never broken. The allied success as the war progressed depended, in part, on their skill in breaking enemy codes; the United States was, for example, able to prepare for the Battle of Midway because it had broken a Japanese code. Such victories would have proven less consequential if the Japanese had simultaneously broken American codes. The idea of using Native American languages as the basis for codes had originated with the Canadian Army, which had relied on Native Americans signaling each other with indigenous languages during World War I. During World War II, the Marine Corps adapted this idea. According to Philip Johnston, who originally urged the implementation of such a code, Native languages offered several advantages, including the fact that few non-Natives spoke any Native languages, and most of them occurred in written form only in anthropological documents. At this time, only 28 Americans who were not Navajo were known to speak Navajo fluently. Because of the wide range of Native languages, they are generally not mutually comprehensible—a Cherokee would not understand any of the Pueblo languages, for example. The code that was eventually created demanded that interpreters knew both English and Navajo.

This code relied on some Navajo words used metaphorically to designate common military terms. The word "da-ha-tih-hi," which means hummingbird in Navajo, was chosen to designate "fighter plane." Much of the code depended on spelling out English words using a particular Navajo word for each letter. Because some English letters such as "e," "s," "r," and "t" occur so often, more than one Navajo word was chosen to indicate those letters. Although this code was not utilized frequently, it did prove effective during some crucial battles, including Okinawa and Iwo Jima.

As occurred with members of other minority groups, readjustment to civilian life did not always come easily to Native Americans. For the first time in their lives, many left their reservations for an extended period. After the war, some returned to a traditional lifestyle, while others pursued more lucrative employment in major cities. Like many African American soldiers and sailors, Native Americans returned to a postwar United States having experienced a greater sense of racial equality overseas. That experience would increase their determination to win the battles for civil rights that would occur with increasing frequency in the generations following World War II.

The following documents provide insight into several aspects of World War II and the development and use of the atomic bomb. Included first is President Roosevelt's response to the attack on Pearl Harbor, in which he asks Congress to declare war against Japan. Next, two documents describe personal experiences of the war in the Pacific. Following this, several documents discuss the atomic bomb—eyewitness accounts of the test at Trinity site, President Truman's thoughts about the use of the bomb as he recorded them in his diary, and reports discussing the advantages and disadvantages of actual use of the bomb as a military weapon. This section concludes with the key to the code used by the Navajo Code Talkers.

PRESIDENT ROOSEVELT'S REQUEST FOR WAR

In the following speech, President Roosevelt, who had served as president through the Great Depression and who would serve an unprecedented four terms, informs the American people of the attack on Pearl Harbor and urges Congress to declare war against Japan. Congress did pass such a declaration later that same day. Roosevelt utters one of his most famous phrases in the opening line: "...a date which will live in infamy." He implies that Japan has acted disingenuously by participating in discussions about peace while planning for war. Although he is not specific about the number of Americans who were killed in this attack—probably because he doesn't yet know—he clearly acknowledges that the attack has been devastating.

Roosevelt's tone is determined. He exercises his leadership not by suggesting that Americans have little to worry about, but rather by expressing his confidence that Americans will respond courageously to Japan's challenge. Simultaneously, he assures the country that he has exercised his power as Commander-in-Chief of the armed services, implying that a military response against Japan is imminent. The last several sentences of the speech aim to convince the nation and the world that the United States will persevere in the face of adversity, that American fortitude and firmness of spirit guarantee an eventual victory. Although Roosevelt's speech is not directly referred to in *Ceremony*, Rocky (and likely some of the other veterans) enlisted, in part, because statements such as these appealed to his pride.

FROM FRANKLIN D. ROOSEVELT, "MESSAGE ASKING FOR WAR AGAINST JAPAN," DECEMBER 8, 1941

(*The Public Papers of F.D. Roosevelt,* Vol. 10, p. 514)

Yesterday, December 7, 1941—a date which will live in infamy—the United States of America was suddenly and deliberately attacked by naval and air forces of the Empire of Japan.

The United States was at peace with that nation and, at the solicitation of Japan, was still in conversation with its Government and its Emperor looking toward the maintenance of peace in the Pacific. Indeed, one hour after Japanese air squadrons had commenced bombing in Oahu, the Japanese Ambassador to the United States and his colleague delivered to the Secretary of State a formal reply to a recent American message. While this reply stated that it seemed useless to continue the existing diplomatic negotiations, it contained no threat or hint of war or armed attack.

It will be recorded that the distance of Hawaii from Japan makes it obvious that the attack was deliberately planned many days or even weeks ago. During the intervening time the Japanese Government has deliberately sought to deceive the United States by false statements and expressions of hope for continued peace.

The attack yesterday on the Hawaiian Islands has caused severe damage to American naval and military forces. Very many American lives have been lost. In addition American ships have been reported torpedoed on the high seas between San Francisco and Honolulu.

Yesterday, the Japanese Government also launched an attack against Malaya. Last night Japanese forces attacked Hong Kong. Last night Japanese forces attacked Guam. Last night Japanese forces attacked the Philippine Islands. Last night the Japanese attacked Wake Island. This morning the Japanese attacked Midway Island.

Japan has, therefore, undertaken a surprise offensive extending throughout the Pacific area. The facts of yesterday speak for themselves. The people of the United States have already formed their opinions and well understand the implications to the very life and safety of our nation.

As Commander-in-Chief of the Army and Navy, I have directed that all measures be taken for our defense.

Always will we remember the character of the onslaught against us.

No matter how long it may take us to overcome this premeditated invasion, the American people in their righteous might will win through to absolute victory.

I believe I interpret the will of the Congress and of the people when I assert that we will not only defend ourselves to the uttermost but will make very certain that this form of treachery shall never endanger us again.

Hostilities exist. There is no blinking at the fact that our people, our territory and our interests are in grave danger.

With confidence in our armed forces—with the unbounded determination of our people—we will gain the inevitable triumph   so help us God.

I ask that the Congress declare that since the unprovoked and dastardly attack by Japan on Sunday, December seventh, a state of war has existed between the United States and the Japanese Empire.

PERSONAL RESPONSES TO THE WAR IN THE PACIFIC

The next two documents describe the experiences of two men who were personally engaged in war. While *Ceremony* places more emphasis on the effects of Tayo's war experiences than it does on his actual time in the service, the following documents describe in more detail what those experiences were like. Art Shedd, particularly, conveys the tedium and the terror of military life. Many of the major battles in World War II claimed thousands of lives, and Japanese defenses, particularly, were so well fortified that allied troops on the front lines knew that casualty rates would be exceptionally high—and individual soldiers knew, entering a battle, that they would likely not survive. Because so many of the battles in the Pacific occurred on islands, assaults were especially difficult strategically and mechanically; sneak attacks were virtually impossible. In addition, Japanese soldiers and even civilians were known to resist surrender much more fiercely than German or Italian soldiers, hence forcing greater sacrifice from the allies. A generation later, Philip Red Eagle fought in the Vietnam War, an experience he draws from in his own writing. In the interview with him that follows, he discusses the racism he experienced as a Native American soldier in addition to other stresses caused or compounded by war.

Art Shedd's Experience

Art Shedd served in the navy during World War II. The following document, edited from a conversation recorded in Delhi, New York, in August 2003, provides a firsthand account of the experiences of a naval officer who participated in the invasion of Normandy—an extended battle that resulted in profound numbers of casualties—and then also served in the Pacific during the last weeks of the war. He provides insight into the common feelings of many sailors—from boredom to dread—as well as the type of pressure experienced by officers. The horrors he witnessed provide additional insight into Tayo's wartime experience, and the loyalty among his men corresponds to the concern for Tayo expressed by other soldiers in *Ceremony*. He also describes the mechanical complexity of different types of ships. Like many Americans who shared his experience, he expresses loyalty to and appreciation for the men who served with him. He also describes the relief his men felt as the war concluded, relief that they had survived and could resume their lives with their families back home.

FROM ART SHEDD (FORMER U.S. NAVAL OFFICER),
TAPE RECORDING, AUGUST 2003, "EXPERIENCE
AS A NAVAL OFFICER"

(Recorded by Lynn Domina)

I was in college during the war, and I went down to Boston and enlisted. In my case
that was a problem initially because I had been born in Canada of American parents,
so the Petty Officer said, "You're not native born. You can't be an officer." So I went
back and my mother got on the phone to the state attorney general. He wrote a letter and I took it down, and they said, "sure," and I was in. I went to Columbia to mid-
shipman's school, and there I became a ninety-day wonder and then went to Little
Creek. You went on board a landing craft, and you were the green crew. The other
guy had been there three weeks; he was now the expert. He left after three weeks and
you became the expert, and you were out on night maneuvers in the Chesapeake Bay.
Fortunately I had been a math major, so navigation and that stuff was easy for me.

I was assigned to an outfit that was going to Europe via England. I was in the invasion on Omaha Beach on D-Day in Normandy. Before the invasion, we were in
port waiting and they took us up to a summer house for some very wealthy people,
and it had a big open room. They had built in that room a model of Omaha Beach,
and they had it to scale. I still remember this. They said to us, "This morning the Germans dragged something across the beach with horses. We don't know what they were
dragging. But we know they did." After we looked at the fortifications, with these
guns in place, I went back to the ship. The ship was sealed—you could write letters,
but you couldn't mail them. Everything was secret. I wrote my wife. I wrote my best
friend and said it doesn't look like I'm going to make this, so if something happens to
me, will you try to look out for her. I thought we were going to be slaughtered.

We were laying off the beach. I had a great crew. We had binoculars, so we could see
what was going on. Ships were in flames. It was not good. The Germans had overlapping
fire. What I mean by that is they had a cement reinforced concrete post facing the water,
but on the side they'd have the openings for the guns to stick out, so they were firing overlapping down the beaches. Anything coming in to hit the pill box would bounce off it
unless you could get up and in there. The Americans had not penetrated when we hit the
beach; they were still trying to get up. The Germans still had control of the highlands.
We were lying off the beach in a large slow circle and this guy came along on what we
call an LCVP. He had a bullhorn and he yelled, "All those who are not yellow, hit the
beach now." I remember those words forever. And I thought, you SOB. You're not going
to the beach. I remember that so clearly. It's a funny thing; it sticks in your mind.

We were going into the beach and I was very busy because the way an LCT works
is you go in, hit the beach, and you drop the ramp. Sometimes you'll hit sand because
it's shallow. What they teach you is that there's a surge of water right after you initially

stop. It tends to lift the craft up, and you gun it and you slide in closer, although we didn't really feel like we wanted to get much closer. In this case we wanted to be sure we got out. We had a big anchor, as big as you'd have on a cruiser, which you dropped as you were going in. You had to be careful because when you got ready to come off the beach, if you used the anchor and reversed the propellers, you'd suck the sand in and, bingo, you'd lose your motors. So you got pulled off the beach initially, as you got your motors going. Just as soon as you got a little space, you backed out, turned around and got out of there.

We were very lucky. Germans bracketed us on the way in. The next shell hit the tank deck and wounded one of the fellows, but we didn't get hit again. We got in and unloaded and got out. By the time we got out, they had hospital ships out there. We blinked the hospital ships, but they already were full and couldn't take any more. So they sent us off to an LST, Landing Ship Tank, which is a landing craft of about 300 feet, a very good target. Put a shell in the middle of them and they'll go down because they're just a hollow shell. It was terrible, dead bodies floating in the water when we were coming back out. There was a breakwater, and the Germans didn't destroy it thank God, and some of the men got behind the breakwater and that saved some of them. When you look back on it, it's amazing we made it through. We paid a heavy price, but there wasn't any other way of doing it.

After that, we were in a bad storm in Normandy which wrecked the beach and actually did a lot of damage to my ship. We were smashed up pretty bad from the storm, not the invasion—we had minor damage from that. During the invasion, we had all kinds of shrapnel on the deck, and I put the guys to work sweeping it up afterwards because I didn't want them thinking about what they'd just been through. Instead, I figured if they got mad at me that was all right; we had to get that stuff cleaned up. They were upset because this buddy of theirs was wounded. When we got ready to go in the invasion, we had been assigned some people who were really in central command and we happened to get a pharmacist's mate thank God, so he was with us. We were on our way in and this fellow got wounded and he was down. Somebody yelled at me, "he's bleeding badly." I was giving commands, getting ready to drop the anchor. We were lining up to go and I really couldn't do much about that. We were yelling "Medic, Medic" but the guy didn't appear. Haygood, my quartermaster who was standing near relaying commands from me when to drop the ramp, when to drop the anchor, and all that—everybody had headphones on—yelled at me, "Skipper, he's [the medic] hiding behind the flag bed," which was right behind us around the corner where the pilot house was. "He's on the back side of it." I remember saying, "Haygood, count to three and if he doesn't go, tell him he has to." And I still remember, he was a southerner, he said, "Yes, sir, did you hear the skipper?" He says, "one" and the guy went zooming across and he saved the fellow's life, he really did. He got bandages on his stomach immediately, slowed down the bleeding. We make these decisions very fast, and you don't have any choice, but you have to do something.

We were brought back to England, in what they call a landing ship dock. It can handle three LCT's—they open the end of it, flood it with water, pull them in, and then they pump the water out. I spent the summer in England, then went back to France, running up and down the coast unloading. I was out of LeHavre most of the time.

Then I was brought home, and I was told I was going to be a training officer on the east coast, but when I got back, I had 30 days proceed time to the South Pacific. I went to Hollandia in New Guinea, and there we were transferred to an LST. The fellows who had been in Europe wouldn't sleep below decks because we were going unescorted. An LST is very very slow. I really do think a submarine on the surface could catch it.

When I went to the Pacific I was made the executive officer of the flotilla which meant that I was the number two man in command. The bad part of that is that when you're a skipper of your own ship, you're busy conning it. You're busy with stuff on board. When you get to be an executive officer of a flotilla, you have personnel who are doing just about everything. There isn't anything for you to do. And I'm telling you the Pacific is no place to be when you don't have anything to do. Awful boring. The one good thing about this was that when I came out to the Pacific, the military was doing a rotation. They were sending fellows back who had been out there for a long time. It was just my misfortune that I had finished up in Europe, so I was an experienced combat officer so they shipped me out there. It was very easy for me with the different ships because I knew none of them had been in actual combat. They'd been running around the Pacific. So the officers and men accepted me because I was experienced. Enlisted men really took care of me. They were so good to me all the time.

We went up to the Philippines to Subic Bay. They were fighting down in Manila at the time, and the Americans were trying to take the land between Subic Bay which had been a big American naval base before the war. They were having difficulty with the Japanese. They wouldn't surrender—you had to kill them, but that finally quieted down, and we were in Subic Bay. Then we were ordered up from the Philippines to Okinawa. This was after the invasion of Okinawa, so we didn't have any combat. And then eventually, we were still in the Philippines when they dropped the A-bombs. And our attitude was thank God they did. Otherwise we'd have to invade Japan, and after what we'd been through in Normandy on Omaha Beach, we knew there were going to be a lot of casualties, so we were happy they did it. We weren't very sympathetic to the Japanese at the time. We were then sent to Kure, Japan, where the Japanese had a naval base like our Annapolis. If I remember correctly, it had to be on an island because our army had established a hospital on it, and there was no way to get to it and get off. So they had to use landing craft to take over supplies. Everything had to be carried over.

Everyone wanted to get home, but the good part was some of them had enough credits to go home, so the others knew they'd be going too. The Japs had surrendered, so we were so relieved that we weren't going to be killed, that we weren't going to be in combat anymore. I think that was the overriding thing. Everybody knew they were going to get home. When I got enough points to be shipped home, I flew on a navy bomber, slow as a freight train, terribly slow. We got to Tokyo—I was the only one on it besides the crew. When you cut back the engine, this thing dropped just like a stone.

We got it down and brought it into the water; it was an amphibious craft so it landed in the water. I disembarked—I was hoping to have a couple of days to look around Tokyo. I went up to the people I had to report to, and the guy said to me, "Oh you're in luck. We got a baby flattop going back. It's going to leave tonight. We'll get you transportation and get you on it right now." I never saw any of Tokyo, just got on the flattop and went back.

They had a deck that went up and down to lift the planes and they had a basket-ball court. We played basketball on the way home. I was up for a lay-up, and the ship rolled and I came down and really did a heck of a job on my ankle, really tore it. So we got to the West Coast—I think I came into L.A.—and I was on crutches. I felt like a damn fool. Complete fool. But there was nothing I could do about it. I got off the ship there and came back to the East Coast on a train. By this time, I had this daughter whom I hadn't seen calling me "Daddy" because her mother had her kiss my picture every night in uniform.

I think I was in the Pacific about twelve months; I was in the navy about three years and some days. I came home; my mother couldn't understand why I wanted to get to work right away. I said I'd been sitting out there doing nothing for the last year.

I was offered the chance when I was in Japan to earn another stripe if I would stay in because they needed trained leaders for the kind of stuff that I had been in. I thought about it—for about two seconds—and that was all. I thought I would take my chances going back. I thought I would go to grad school because they had the G.I. Bill. I didn't know where that would lead, but I thought I'll be my own boss rather than being told what to do.

Philip Red Eagle's Experience in Vietnam

Philip Red Eagle is a writer of Dakota and Puget Sound Salish heritage. He writes poetry, fiction, and essays, and is best known for a pair of novellas published as *Red Earth: A Vietnam Warrior's Journey.* He credits Leslie Marmon Silko as someone who has provided much support for his own writing. As he states in the following interview, he was unaware of traditional ceremonies intended to reincorporate warriors into civil society when he returned from Vietnam; however, he has since come to understand their value. Because the nature of war has changed so dramatically since the beginning of the twentieth century, demanding the presence of tens of thousands (rather than dozens or hundreds) of soldiers, traditional ceremonies offered on a broad scale are probably logistically impossible. In the following interview, conducted via e-mail during January 2004, Red Eagle discusses his experiences in the military as well as his goals and concerns as a writer.

FROM PHILIP RED EAGLE

(Interview by Lynn Domina, January 2004)

Q: Many Native American writers, yourself included (more than non–Native [American] writers), write in more than one genre and/or practice writing along with at least one other art form. Could you comment on how you see poetry and prose as interacting? To what extent are the roles or purposes of the two genres different?

Red Eagle: I feel that many of my own characters are poets as they live out the lives and adventures that form around them. It is their poetry which finds its way into my tales. I think it is more true in my more recent writings as I delve into sci-fi, or Native American sci-fi. My characters tend to speak in poetry; their words flow out in poetic form, or at least a free-form style of poetry. I find myself writing in this way, and what comes out emerges from both me and the character that I am attempting to build.

This is also true of the poetry that I have written. The poetry in me seems to find its own way out in spite of having me in the way. This November when my mother died, I found myself realizing more about her than I had realized before her death. The reason I did not see this other person was that her living-self was in the way. I think that this is true with the poetry which comes from that someone inside of me and forces it out past the me that I know, that which is in the way. I think that this is why it comes out so complete. I rarely rewrite, or edit, the words—as they are finished as they emerge.

My view of prose and poetry is that they are small stems shooting from the same branch; they are actually not that different, or distinct, from the other. This is the same with all "art." After all, the "art" voice is an extension of our emotion. Emotion is part and parcel of being a human being. Being a human being is the art. I think this is why I shift from one art form to another. I do not distinguish one from the other; neither is the exception to the other.

Q: How do you aim to incorporate strategies from the oral traditions into written texts?

Red Eagle: I do not "aim" to incorporate anything. I do not differentiate between the "oral" tradition and the "written" tradition. Some say there is a difference. I do not see it. I tell a tale with my voice, or I tell a tale with my pen (or computer). Of course, there is the structure which appears when writing, but it is basically the same as the voice projections—at least at first. As I tell a story it is being formed by whom I am telling the story to, and the conditions in which I am telling that story. Lately, I have been telling this one "Blue Jay" story over and over. I have told it about five times. Each telling took its own shape, yet the point of the story remained the same. For instance, I told this story to a small intimate audience at a party; the next telling was during an Inipi Ceremony (sweat) to a group of veterans. Laughing is always appropriate. The next was on a stage using a [microphone] to an audience, as opposed to a group of friends. The next was to a friend in an office. The next, standing outside of the Washington State History Museum in Tacoma with four people that I had worked with on an exhibit there. I was delivering a request for payment to someone in the building. As I was looking for a parking spot, I noticed these four people standing outside the back door. They were actually talking in two groups of two. One person was smoking. I yelled out of the truck window a remark about "smoking and joking on government time." He yelled back that they did not have a joke and that I should provide one. I parked nearby and joined two and the other two joined us. I told this Blue Jay story in a short, joke, form. They laughed and understood as if I had just told them the whole story with its gestures, faces, dialogue, and sounds. I do not intend to write this story because it has already existed for a long time in its oral state, going from one person to another without ever having been written. I heard it from a friend while riding the Washington State Ferry from Everett to Whidbey Island. If you don't know already, Blue Jay is the trickster character of the Salish people who have resided here in Puget Sound for several thousand years. I have not written this story down and really do not intend to. I wish to see it continue in its present form, just as flexible and stretchable as it has always been. Yet, I will use the context of the story in a written tale; disguised, but to serve the same purpose.

Q: *The character of Clifford in "Bois de Sioux" and you yourself in other interviews have defined a warrior as "one who serves the people." Can you elaborate on why the role of warrior is a service? How is the service of a warrior different from, say, the service of a person who belongs to a medicine society?*

Red Eagle: Well, over the many years that these various Native American nations have existed, there were times of friction with neighboring nations, or even with related tribes. I feel that migration and resources are always a factor. It was during these times of friction that warriors, as such, would become necessary. The need for violence would ultimately, but not always, rise to the surface of a dispute. There were always the games and competitions which would decide who used what resources, and when, before violence would ever become a factor. It was really no different when the Europeans arrived on the scene. Migration and the need for resources, or the desire for more resources, always came to play. So, at times, warriors became as necessary as medicine men and women, and as vital as those who gather, or cultivate, these resources. Of course, you do not want two things to happen: one, the warriors take over the tribal process, in which case it is not tribal anymore; two, the warriors step outside the bounds of good conduct within the tribal structure, i.e., those whom violence has changed, or altered, so much as to have become a danger to "the people." As we have recently learned from our experiences in Vietnam, violence and trauma tend to alter one's perspective on the world and community and one's conduct within one's society, or tribe. The first is sometimes not preventable. The changes in the Iroquois society over long contact with the European arrivals are a good example. The Iroquoian ventures into the West to gather territory in the late 1700s has been historically noted. They abandoned the normal tribal structure, warrior conduct, and family, and formed a large army which ravaged much of the region in the southwestern Great Lakes region in order to gain access to fur-bearing animals for trade with the whites. They were only stopped by the Dakota as they attempted a move into what is now Minnesota and Iowa.

In regard to the former, in which conduct is altered, the elders, in regard to the wisdom of tradition, would cut this bad conduct off by introducing a process which would prevent such contrary acts. This process was marked by several layers of previolence ceremony, in which the warrior-to-be would be taught to understand that he, or she, was entering into a mind-altering, spirit-altering, experience that could have serious implications upon return to "the people." After such violence, the warrior would be subjected to more ceremonies which slowed the warrior's reentry into the family and the tribe. The warriors would be held out of the village for several days. During that time he would tell his particular story to his peers. Each would tell their story, in turn, until all was told. Then the cleansing ceremonies would begin. These ceremonies would begin with the Inipi Ceremony and evolve through the washing of hands and hair and the thorough cleansing of the physical self. Last would be the "formal" entry into the village by procession, and then each warrior would be seated in the center and be given the opportunity to tell his story once more, with the support of his immediate family, to the whole village. It was only after all of these stories were told that the warriors would be allowed into the village. Then there would be feasting and dancing to honor these warriors and thank them for their sacrifice. Then there would be layers of ceremonial conduct added to the healing process. For instance, required entry into one or more warriors' societies in which one's conduct would be set and monitored. This was a lot of effort for the tribe, but in the long run, it was well worth it.

Q: Did your experience in Vietnam confirm this understanding of the warrior?

Red Eagle: No! I had no idea about any of this ceremonial process and conduct. At least upon my return. All this was absent. It took 20 years to acquire this understanding. I did not put any of this together until long after my return home. And, after entering counseling via the Vets Center in Seattle. In fact, becoming a "warrior" was never a factor until recently when I began to participate in the Inipi Ceremony back in late 1992. It was only after entering this process did I begin to understand the role of the warrior. Those of us who went overseas back then learned some things that we cannot discard, nor forget. Understanding the role of the "warrior" actually eased the grief of that time. Also, understanding that what I participated in had "another meaning" made a big difference in the healing process, as well.

Q: People (and literary characters) join the military for a number of different reasons, patriotism being only one, and they often have mixed motives. In Silko's novel, Ceremony, *for instance, Tayo enlists in part because Rocky refers to him as his "brother." Why did you enlist? Why the navy specifically?*

Red Eagle: I enlisted to avoid the draft. I suppose that many of us did that. If the draft got you, you could then be processed into any service. With enlistment you could decide what service and in what capacity you would serve. I chose the navy to satisfy my mother. She had brothers, cousins, and uncles go off to the Marine Corps and the army to fight in the Pacific Theater during World War II. She saw them come back and the condition of their arrival; or she saw them *not* come back. She wanted us out of harm's way. Of course, when I was In-Country Vietnam, on the river, I did not tell her exactly where I was or what I was doing when I wrote home. She assumed that I was offshore, and I did not let her know any different. I never did really tell her and she never asked.

Q: Was there any single experience that encapsulates your experience in Vietnam?

Red Eagle: I suppose I could narrow it down to the first time we got "hit," or the time I almost killed, or gunned down, an officer near the end of my tour. He was a racist and was making racist remarks to my black (African American) patrol partner and me. Actually, more toward me, it seemed. It was my black partner who saved him, or kept me from shooting him. I was on duty at the time. We had many duties while In-Country. Of course, everything is escalated because of the presence of war all the time. This village patrol thing was very much like being a policeman. Except that it was a war and everyone was crazy because of it.

Earlier that night there was a shoot-out between factions on the street of the ville. Of course, we did not know who or what these factions were at that time. It turned out to be between an army soldier and some Vietnamese soldiers. M-16s were going off. Everyone headed for cover. It was dark; pitch black, one might say. We could not see anything, except the occasional gunfire flashes. Soon the gunfire stopped and flashlights appeared. One of the army patrols took charge (we shared duty with the other services). The parties were picked up and hauled away. As always, we were informed later about what had happened, but we never did learn the result of the action. I mean, if someone died, or if there were several deaths. During this incident Alton and myself dove behind a large water barrel. I jammed a clip into my .45 caliber handgun (Colt, 1911) and loaded a round into the chamber. I never did lock (engage the safety) that night. When the incident was over, I just eased the hammer down, slipped the gun into my holster and forgot about it. Our duty was to patrol the street (it was only one street) and the bars, and keep order (yeah, like order in chaos). We would pull this duty once or twice a month. There was lots to do, including movement security and static security on the river. And defense. We entered the last bar on the street. I started talking with one of the bar girls. Then this guy started bad-mouthing me. I suppose he had some connection with this girl. It was pretty bad. You know, I cannot remember the exact words. It was like "niggers" and "red-nigger" kind of talk. Before I knew what was going on, I had my gun pointed right at his chest. Alton said, "Don't do it, brother. He ain't worth it." He put his hand over my wrist and moved my arm downward. I moved the gun aside, from under Alton's hand, and raised it to the officer (I just then recognized the bars on his lapel). I was going to pull the trigger, but the bar girl jumped in front of him and then stepped to me and wrapped her arms around me. She was screaming something. I stepped back and tried to wriggle out of her grip. She said, "Don't do it. Please, don't do it." I put my arms to my side and stepped off a few steps. I holstered the gun. Alton stepped to me and grabbed my left arm and turned me toward the door. "Let's go, brother! He ain't worth it!"

With all the things that happened over those three years overseas, why does this stand out? I suppose that it was the contrariness of it. The issue of personal honor being another reason: shooting down an unarmed man over the issue of race. Most do not understand that there was another war going on over there then, about race. The United States was having a race war at home, and it reflected itself in the war in Vietnam. So complex; an officer corps that seemed to be racist. Especially, In-Country, in the field. War is crazy enough. These added dimensions made it even more so.

Q: You've spoken about Native [American] practices of reincorporating warriors into society. Did you participate in any healing ceremonies when you returned to the United States after your enlistment? Do you think such practices would be possible on a large scale—that is, with the participation of the number of soldiers who tend to fight in contemporary wars? Do you have suggestions for veterans for whom such practices are not part of their cultural tradition?

Red Eagle: For the most part, these ceremonies were not in wide practice in those days, and most returning Native American servicemen had no inkling that such things existed. These days, it is much different. I attend the Inipi quite regularly. In fact, I lead a "sweat" for veterans on the Puyallup reservation. I do not see "us" conducting these ceremonies for the amount of men and women who are currently involved in Iraq and Afghanistan. The only way for it to be possible would be to let it go and basically release it into open use by any number of unqualified persons to run such ceremonies. I don't think that it would work. I had "sweat" for seven years before it even occurred to me that I should conduct the ceremony for other vets. I suggest that those who have the opportunity to participate in these ceremonies should take it. It seems an odd proposal, but one that should be accepted. We accept any vet, regardless of race, color or creed, into our lodge. Our interest is to serve the vet, regardless.

Q: As Silko does in Ceremony, *you focus more on the veterans' return in* Red Earth *than on their actual wartime experiences. Reentry into civilian society seems more*

compelling, at least psychologically and spiritually, than the actual time set apart
for war. Why is that?

Red Eagle: The contrast! When you are at war, these things are not at issue. Survival and success in combat are at the fore. When you get home, you only wish to become immersed back into your old life, thinking that you want all the things that you wanted before going to war. Of course, you have no idea that you have changed so radically. So much so, that it is said that the person who left for war is basically gone, dead. A stranger has returned; another person. This person cannot get past the experience of war and in actuality will bear the burden of that war for the rest of his life. The homogeneous return to society does not exist.

Q: In some ways, Tayo seems to fit the stereotype of the Vietnam veteran better than he does the stereotype of the World War II veteran. Certainly, many veterans of World War II suffered from "battle fatigue," though their experiences were perhaps less public than the experiences of veterans of Vietnam with posttraumatic stress. Do you think the experiences of soldiers in the two wars was dramatically different, or is it only our ideas that are different—and perhaps misguided?

Red Eagle: War is the same in any time and any place. War takes the same toll. There is no difference between the "warrior" returning home from battle with the neighboring tribe and the soldier who returns from Iraq.

Q: In Ceremony, *Tayo sees Uncle Josiah in the Japanese soldiers he is ordered to execute. In your novellas, characters also exist in times and places that aren't realistically possible. Do notions of the "real" simply indicate a lack of vision? Are there spiritual truths that can only be understood through a suspension of "reality"?*

Red Eagle: What is reality? When first starting on these stories, I started with my experiences, or what I thought were my experiences. I realized, of course, that for me, my story was actually quite boring and of no consequence when stated in a "real" way. It was then that I started talking to my Vietnam vet friends. I also remembered a little story that was told to me in the Inipi by a Lakota man from Rosebud. He was telling me a version of "White Buffalo Calf Woman" that I had not heard before. He said that a man he knew to be a medicine man had told him this version. In this version, after the woman had taken the young man who desired her away into this whirling cloud and then returned in what seemed like moments later standing beside this pile of bones, she consoled the remaining young man by telling him this: "Oh, do not worry over these bones of your friend. He desired me, and as his reward for finding me here, I took him away to another place far from here where we married, had children and grandchildren and stayed with one another for a long and happy life. These bones you see here are the bones of an old man who led a long life and died happily. Now, I will give you your reward. Because you did not desire me, but looked upon me with respect, and because you are a person who thinks only of serving his people, I have this for you." She proceeded to unveil her story and gifted to the people, in his name, the Sacred Pipe and all the rules and ceremonies that come with it. It was in this version of the story that I saw time travel as a spiritual reality. Of course, only special, and very powerful, people can accomplish this type of movement through time and space. So, I developed my characters so that they became these special people.

There are those who have "flashbacks" (most of us). For these men, these flashbacks are as real as the actual event; and, in fact, they believe they are in the actual, or original, event. Is that real? When I first started attending the University of Washington, Seattle, back in 1976, I was merely three years out of my experiences in Vietnam. I had these hard-soled boots that I used to like to wear. But, there were several surfaces on campus in which my hard-soled boots made the exact sound that my jungle boots made on that little blacktop piece of road in the ville. In that moment I could smell, hear, and taste Vietnam. At least the piece of Vietnam that I was in.

What's real? Who really knows?

WITNESSES TO THE ATOMIC BOMB TEST

The next four documents describe the experience of witnessing the successful test of an atomic bomb at Trinity Site in New Mexico. Because so much time and money had been spent creating the bomb, these scientists were both excited and relieved that the test was successful. They tend to describe the explosion in fairly objective terms, although they also rely on figurative language because metaphors and similes, such as the common description of a "mushroom cloud," are often the only means available to describe a totally new experience. Their challenge was to convey the explosion adequately to an audience who had never witnessed anything like it. In *Ceremony*, when Tayo's grandmother witnesses the test, she doesn't know quite how to describe it either. While this test certainly had political and military effects, these witnesses are primarily concerned with the scientific nature of the bomb. The descriptions are similar in several ways, but each author adopts a unique style and emphasizes different aspects of the test.

The Account of L. W. Alvarez

L. W. Alvarez witnessed the test from an airplane several miles away from the actual bomb site. Nevertheless, he was able to describe the event quite graphically, especially in visual terms. He mentions his initial confusion about how many red balls he saw, and though he initially thought he saw three different balls of fire, he later decided that he must have seen the same ball from three different angles; the cloud cover prevented him from watching it constantly. Given how quickly the event transpired, his confusion is reasonable. He estimates that the cloud rose about 40,000 feet in the air, or nearly eight miles. He mentions that he did not feel the shock of the explosion though he might have expected to, even at such a distance.

FROM L. W. ALVAREZ, "AN EYE-WITNESS ACCOUNT
OF THE TRINITY SHOT ON MONDAY MORNING
AT 5:30 A.M. 16 JULY 1945"

(U.S. National Archives, Record Group 227, OSRD-S1 Committee, Box 82,
Folder 6, "Trinity")

I was kneeling between the pilot and co-pilot in B-29 No. 384 and observed the explosion through the pilot's window on the left side of the plane. We were about 20 to 25 miles from the site and the cloud cover between us and the ground was approximately 7/10. About 30 seconds before the object was detonated the clouds obscured our vision of the point so that we did not see the initial stages of the ball of fire. I was looking through crossed polaroid [*sic*] glasses directly at the site. My first sensation was one of intense light covering my whole field of vision. This seemed to last for about 1/2 second after which I noted an intense orange red glow through the clouds. Several seconds later it appeared that a second spherical red ball appeared but it is probable that this apparent phenomenon was caused by the motion of the airplane bringing us to a position where we could see through the cloud directly at the ball of fire which had been developing for the past few seconds. This fire ball seemed to have a rough texture with irregular black lines dividing the surface of the sphere into a large number of small patches of reddish orange. This thing disappeared a few seconds later and what seemed to be a third ball of fire appeared again and I am now convinced that this was all the same fire ball which I saw on two separate occasions through a new hole in the undercast.

When this "third ball" disappeared the light intensity dropped considerably and within another 20 seconds or so the cloud started to push up through the undercast. It first appeared as a parachute which was being blown up by a large electric fan. After the hemispherical cap had emerged through the cloud layer one could see a cloud of smoke about 1/3 the diameter of the "parachute" connecting the bottom of the hemisphere with the undercast. This had very much the appearance of a large mushroom. The hemispherical structure was creased with "longitude lines" running from the pole to the equator. In another minute the equatorial region had partially caught up with the poles giving a flattened out appearance to the top of the structure. In the next few minutes the symmetry of the structure was broken up by wind currents at various altitudes so the shape of the cloud cannot be described in any geometrical manner. In about 8 minutes the top of the cloud was at approximately 40,000 feet as close as I could estimate from our altitude of 24,000 feet and this seemed to be the maximum altitude attained by the cloud. I did not feel the shock wave hit the plane but the pilot felt the reaction on the rudder through the rudder pedals. Some of the other passengers in the plane noted a rather small shock at the time but it was not apparent to me.

The Account of Kenneth Greisen

Closer to the actual site than L. W. Alvarez, Kenneth Greisen observed the explosion from the ground, even lying down to avoid any injury. Greisen describes feeling anxious because he might have been responsible if any mechanical failure had occurred. He observes the explosion through welding glass in order to protect his eyes from the glare. Greisen describes both his own emotional response and also the jubilant responses of the men around him. Although he does feel the shock wave and describes it as lasting for some time, he is much more impressed with the bomb's visual display. He concludes by describing the dispersal of the mushroom cloud, which also took longer than he expected.

FROM KENNETH GREISEN, "EYE-WITNESS ACCOUNT OF
TRINITY SHOT," 1945

(U.S. National Archives, Record Group 227, OSRD-S1
Committee, Box 82, Folder 6, "Trinity")

A group of us were lying on the ground just outside of base camp (10 miles from the charge), and received time signals over the radio, warning us when the shot would occur. I was personally nervous, for my group had prepared and installed the detonators, and if the shot turned out to be a dud, it might possibly be our fault. We were pretty sure we had done our job well, but there is always some chance of a slip.

At minus about 15 seconds I put my head close to the ground, turned to look away from the tower, and put up a shield between my head and the tower. I probably also closed my eyes briefly just before the shot. Suddenly I felt heat on the side of my head toward the tower, opened my eyes and saw a brilliant yellow-white light all around. The heat and light were as though the sun had just come out with unusual brilliance. About a second later I turned to look at the tower through the dark welding glass. A tremendous cloud of smoke was pouring upwards, some parts having brilliant red and yellow colors, like clouds at sunset. These parts kept folding over and over like dough in a mixing bowl. At this time I believe I exclaimed, "My god, it worked!" and felt a great relief.

When the intensity of the light had diminished, I put away the glass and looked toward the tower directly. At about this time I noticed a blue color surrounding the smoke cloud. Then someone shouted that we should observe the shock wave travelling along the ground. The appearance of this was a brightly lighted circular area, near the ground, slowly spreading out towards us. The color was yellow.

At what I presume was about 50 seconds after the shot, the ground shock and sound reached us almost simultaneously. The noise lasted for a long time, echoing back and forth from the hills. I noticed no sharp crack, but a rumbling sound as of thunder. After the brilliant optical display we had seen, the ground shock and noise were disappointing. No damage occurred, and we were not at all severely shaken.

Between the appearance of light and the arrival of the sound, there was loud cheering in the group around us. After the noise was over, we all went about congratulating each other and shaking hands. I believe we were all much more shaken up by the shot mentally than physically.

The permanence of the smoke cloud was one thing that surprised me. After the first rapid explosion, the lower part of the cloud seemed to assume a fixed shape and to remain hanging motionless in the air. The upper part meanwhile continued to rise, so that after a few minutes it was at least five miles high. It slowly assumed a zigzag shape because of the changing wind velocity at different altitudes. The smoke had pierced a cloud early in its ascent, and seemed to be completely unaffected by the cloud.

The Account of P. Morrison

P. Morrison's account is the most precise of those included here. He aims to provide substantial detail regarding the nature of the explosion. His descriptions are consistent with those of the other observers—he focuses on the intense light and also expresses some disappointment with the shock wave, for example—but he seldom reveals any emotional response. When he does, that revelation is subtle, as when he describes himself huddling close to the ground. He also refers to the bomb as the "gadget," a common description among scientists involved in the project, partly, perhaps, for security reasons, but the term sounds peculiarly innocuous to contemporary ears. He states that he has tried to estimate the brightness of the flash by staring at the sun through protective lenses and concludes that the explosion was several times brighter than the noon sun. His frequent references to time reveal that the entire event took about one minute. Within fifteen minutes, much evidence of the explosion had dispersed.

FROM P. MORRISON, "OBSERVATIONS OF THE TRINITY SHOT JULY 16, 1945"

(U.S. National Archives, Record Group 227, OSRD-S1 Committee, Box 82, Folder 6, "Trinity")

I observed the Trinity shot looking toward Zero from a position on the south bank of the base camp reservoir directly beside the larger water tank. There were three distinct stages in the process I saw, which I describe consecutively as follows:

1. Instantaneous glow and ball of fire

At time T = −45 seconds I lay prone facing Zero wearing ordinary sun glasses and holding in one hand a stop watch and in the other the welding glass issued by the stockroom. I watched the second-hand until T = −5 seconds when I lowered my head onto the sand bank in such a way that a slight rise in the ground completely shielded me from Zero. I placed the welding glass over the right lens of my sun glasses, the left lens of which was covered by an opaque cardboard shield. I counted seconds and at zero began to raise my head just over the protecting rise. During this motion the gadget went off while I was looking at it or possibly a small fraction of a second before. What I saw first was a brilliant violet glow entering my eyes by reflection from the ground and from the surroundings generally. I had not raised my head quite enough to provide a clear vision of Zero. Immediately after this brilliant violet flash, which was somewhat blinding, I observed through the welding glass, centered at the direction of the tower an enormous and brilliant disk of white light. The sensation lasted for such a short time and the light was so great that I cannot be sure of the shape observed. I remember it only as a well-marked vaguely round pattern. This disk was a true white in color, even through the welding glass which makes the sun's disk distinctly deep green. On subsequently looking at the noon sun through these glasses I have been led to estimate this initial stage of the gadget as corresponding to a color much whiter or bluer and a brightness several times greater than that of the noon sun. I felt a strong sensation of heat on the exposed skin of face and arms, lasting for several seconds and at least as intense as the direct noon sun.

It should be noted that my eyes were adapted to twilight or perhaps even to somewhat brighter light because of the use of the radio dial light I had made just previous to the T-45 second signal.

2. Growth of the mushroom

For a time which I guess to be less than two seconds the bright disk produced an after effect in my eyes which spoiled the details of the following process. I quickly realized that my vision was improving, that the image was becoming much fainter and less white. I then took off the welding glass and several seconds later the sun glasses as well. Beginning at T = +2 to 3 seconds, I observed the somewhat yellowed disk beginning to be eaten into from below by dark obscuring matter. Meanwhile the whole surface of the plain was covered with matter being thrown up into the air as the motion continued outward from Zero. In a matter of a few seconds more the disk had nearly stopped growing horizontally and was beginning to extend in a vertical direction while its appearance had transformed into that of a bright glowing distinctly red column of flame mixed with swirling obscuring matter. The column looked rather like smoke and flame rising from an oil fire. This turbulent red column rose straight up several thousand feet in a few seconds growing a mushroom-like head of the same kind. This mushroom was fully developed and the whole glowing structure complete at about 15,000 feet altitude. I do not recall whether this stage was reached before or after the arrival of the shock. At T +30 I realized the shock was due very soon and I huddled closer to the ground in anticipation of a severe shock. The arrival of the air shock at T +45 on my stopwatch came as an anti-climax. I noticed two deep thuds which sounded rather like a kettle drum rhythm being played some distance away. I remember the sound as being without any important high frequency components as cracks, etc. There was no earth tremor perceptible to me at any time. The ground on which I was lying was a very loosely packed dike of mud.

3. Appearance of the smoke cloud

After the passage of the shock I stood up to watch the end of the mushroom. The red glow died out and the mushroom appeared as a column of smoke or cloud hanging over Zero. In a matter of another minute or so the smoke had arranged itself in three rather well defined oblique clouds forming roughly a vertical Z. The lowest cloud was quite well defined, and stretched north at a slight angle. At a couple of thousand feet, it appeared to bend around almost double and to stretch about southeast for a somewhat greater distance. This second cloud again seemed broken off rather sharply and a large cloud gradually spread with less and less well defined shape from the upper end of the second step. This process was nearly complete when the upper cap was spread over most of the bowl at a height of about 30,000 feet. There was a strong impression of definite layers in the wind structure, and there were even some water vapor clouds which seemed to mark the boundaries between winds of different directions. The completion of this stage took many minutes until finally the cloud was rather well dispersed toward north 10,000 at a rather low level, had overspread at an intermediate level all the way to the Oscuro mountains, and on a higher level was drifting slowly south and southeast.

Other observations:

After T = +50 seconds, I distinctly smelled upon standing up a faint but marked odor of ozone or corona discharge ionization.

At T +15 minutes or more I observed Zero through a battery commander's periscope set of 8-power. Not much detail was visible in this region. A sort of dust haze seemed to cover the area. A remarkable amount of heat shimmer was noticed on the horizon directly above the Zero area. It was shortly after this that I saw the Jumbo tower was missing.

Size and distance figures mentioned here are based on judgments of angular size and the assumption of 18,000 yards distance from Zero to base camp.

The Account of Cyril S. Smith

Unlike the other observers here included, Cyril S. Smith questions the wisdom of this invention. He suggests that "we"—the United States, the scientists, the military—might have unleashed a greater power than they anticipated. His statement at the end that a city is no longer a prudent place to live indicates that he assumes this bomb will be used and that cities—crowded residential areas rather than exclusively military installations—will be targets. Because he does not state that cities would not be the place to live specifically for enemies of the United States, he could be assuming that the bomb will eventually be used against the United States, also. He suggests that the initial response of observers was more solemn than jubilant, although they grew more excited as they understood their success. Although he uses slightly different terminology, Smith's description of the physical nature of the explosion is consistent with the other descriptions.

FROM CYRIL S. SMITH, "EYEWITNESS ACCOUNT OF
TRINITY TEST, JULY 16, 1945"

(U.S. National Archives, Record Group 227, OSRD-S1
Committee, Box 82, Folder 6, "Trinity")

I was located at the base camp, behind a five foot embankment near the water tanks at T = 0. I was facing away from the shot, somewhat bent down below the top of the bank. In addition, my eyes were partly covered by a welder's glass. For a time estimated as two seconds (though it may have been less) I was watching the ground through the corner of my eye. Even though this was lighted by reflection from the clouds, it was intensely bright and apparently free from color. Since the shot there has been some discussion of the duration of this intense light, but it is definitely my recollection that I opened and closed my eyes several times and waited for the light to decrease in intensity before turning to face the reaction zone directly. Even after the estimated 2 seconds the light was still intense enough to be clearly seen through the welder's glass but there was no direct ball of fire or structure or any symmetry, this part of the phenomenon evidently having ceased.

The appearance of a turbulent gas apparently undergoing combustion was quite surprising. It looked not much different from the film of the 100 ton shot or any large fire, for instance an oil tank fire or the Graf Zeppelin. After another second or two I removed the welder's glass and looked directly. As the main light became less intense, the bluish ionization zone became visible, extending to a diameter almost twice that of the area where there was incandescence. I noticed a dust cloud travelling near the ground, and at some stage (I am not sure whether early or late in the proceedings, but it was definitely illuminated by the shot) I noticed a ring, supposedly of moisture condensed by the rarefaction wave, at a level slightly below the clouds. This ring did not spread, but once formed seemed to remain stationary.

At the instant after the shot, my reactions were compounded of relief that "it worked"; consciousness of extreme silence, and a momentary question as to whether we had done more than we intended. Practically none of the watchers made any vocal comment until after the shock wave had passed and even then the cheers were not intense or prolonged. The elation of most observers seemed to increase for a period of 30 minutes afterwards, as they had a chance to absorb the significance of the achievement.

The rising of the cloud of reaction products to above the cloud level seems to have proceeded rapidly but in a normal fashion. It was noticeable that there were a number of rough projections, indicating high local turbulence. Shortly after the smoke column with its mushroom top was formed, wind currents distorted it into a jagged or corkscrew appearance. There was a dust cloud over the ground, extending for a considerable distance. A cloud, whether of dust or moisture particles, hung close to the ground and slowly drifted east into the hills, persisting for over an hour.

The obvious fact that all of the reaction products were not proceeding upward in a neat ball but were lagging behind and being blown by low altitude winds over the ground in the direction of inhabited areas produced very definite reflection that this is not a pleasant weapon we have produced. Later reflections were on the manner of defense against it and the realization that a city is henceforth not the place in which to live.

DEBATES ABOUT WHETHER TO USE THE BOMB

Contemporary discussions of whether the United States was right to use the atomic bomb on Japan at the end of World War II often become quite heated, and when the August 6 and 9 anniversaries are acknowledged, the emotional tenor is often mournful. Currently, although many countries are now nuclear powers and although large stockpiles of the weapons exist, many people view the actual potential use of another atomic weapon as a strategy to be avoided at all costs. In part because so many different countries have manufactured nuclear weapons, most assume that any additional use of an atomic bomb would inevitably elicit so much retaliation as to utterly destroy the earth. In *Ceremony*, Old Betonie responds to the use of this bomb and other elements of modern warfare with puzzlement—how can a soldier not witness the enemy he kills? The novel also implies that the development and use of the bomb did more to disrupt the harmony of the world than nearly any other event.

When the bomb was developed, however, the questions of whether and how it should be used seemed much murkier. Although an allied defeat of Japan appeared increasingly likely, military strategists generally suggested that the allies would have to invade Japan in order to achieve an actual surrender. Such an invasion would likely come at the price of thousands of allied lives. Given how many soldiers and sailors had already been killed in the Pacific and in Europe, the United States government sincerely hoped to achieve victory without an invasion. To some, the only other option was to use atomic weapons against Japan. Others argued that additional solutions existed. The decision, however, was no longer an exclusively military one; ethics had entered the conversation since the United States was aware of how devastatingly destructive the bomb would be. Scientists knew that this particular weapon was qualitatively different from any other. Unfortunately, none of the choices available at the time was unequivocally good; as is often the case in wartime, all of the available options were tainted with evil. To the extent that ethics did inform the decision-making process, the challenge was to select the military strategy that would produce the least evil. Perhaps the United States made the correct choice; perhaps not. The one certain fact is that Japan recognized the horror of the bomb, for the Japanese surrendered immediately after its use.

The next three documents debate a number of these issues: Should the bomb be used at all? Should its existence be publicized? Would a threat to use it be sufficient? If it is used, how should targets be determined?

President Truman's Decision

In the diary entry excerpted below, President Truman outlines his decision, made with the Secretary of War, a short two weeks before the bomb was actually used. He describes the results of the test ten days before and himself seems astonished at the bomb's power. Truman's description of how the bomb would be used—against exclusively military targets—proved inaccurate, as the bomb was eventually dropped on two populous cities rather than on military bases or industrial complexes. Truman refers to the Japanese as particularly barbaric, yet suggests that a nation such as the United States must nevertheless resist the temptation to destroy its civilization. Truman admits that the bomb is "terrible," yet suggests that it can still be put to good use.

FROM HARRY S. TRUMAN, DIARY ENTRY (JULY 25, 1945)

http://www.clannen.com/decision/hst-j125.html

We have discovered the most terrible bomb in the history of the world. It may be the fire destruction prophesied in the Euphrates Valley Era, after Noah and his fabulous Ark.

Anyway we "think" we have found the way to cause a disintegration of the atom. An experiment in the New Mexico desert was startling—to put it mildly. Thirteen pounds of the explosive caused the complete disintegration of a steel tower 60 feet high, created a crater 6 feet deep and 1,200 feet in diameter, knocked over a steel tower 1/2 mile away and knocked men down 10,000 yards away. The explosion was visible for more than 200 miles and audible for 40 miles and more.

This weapon is to be used against Japan between now and August 10th. I have told the Sec. of War, Mr. Stimson, to use it so that military objectives and soldiers and sailors are the target and not women and children. Even if the Japs are savages, ruthless, merciless and fanatic, we as the leader of the world for the common welfare cannot drop that terrible bomb on the old capital or the new.

He and I are in accord. The target will be a purely military one and we will issue a warning statement asking the Japs to surrender and save lives. I'm sure they will not do that, but we will have given them the chance. It is certainly a good thing for the world that Hitler's crowd or Stalin's did not discover this atomic bomb. It seems to be the most terrible thing ever discovered, but it can be made the most useful....

Scientists Urge the United States Not to Use the Bomb

The Franck Report, excerpted below, suggests that military use of the bomb in 1945 would prove to be a mistake. The report prophetically suggests that any early use of the weapon will result in an arms race between the United States and any other nation that could eventually develop the weapon. Such a prediction is not far-fetched, the report argues, because scientists throughout the world understand the theory behind nuclear arms; hence, several other countries could be just a few years away from producing an actual weapon.

The report suggests that international regulations regarding the use of atomic weapons be in place before they are used. As significantly, the report defines the atomic bomb as an issue to be addressed over time and within the political, rather than exclusively military, sphere. That is, these scientists urge President Truman and his advisors to consider the long-term political consequences that would likely emerge from the use of such a weapon before a decision to use the bomb is actually reached.

FROM "REPORT OF THE COMMITTEE ON POLITICAL AND SOCIAL PROBLEMS MANHATTAN PROJECT 'METALLURGICAL LABORATORY,'" UNIVERSITY OF CHICAGO, JUNE 11, 1945 (THE FRANCK REPORT). MEMBERS OF THE COMMITTEE: JAMES FRANCK (CHAIRMAN), DONALD J. HUGHES, J. J. NICKSON, EUGENE RABINOWITCH, GLENN T. SEABORG, J. C. STEARNS, LEO SZILARD

(U.S. National Archives, Washington D.C.: Record Group 77, Manhattan Engineer District Records, Harrison-Bundy File, Folder 76)

The development of nuclear power not only constitutes an important addition to the technological and military power of the United States, but also creates grave political and economic problems for the future of this country.

Nuclear bombs cannot possibly remain a "secret weapon" at the exclusive disposal of this country, for more than a few years. The scientific facts on which their construction is based are well known to scientists of other countries. Unless an effective international control of nuclear explosives is instituted, a race of nuclear armaments is certain to ensue following the first revelation of our possession of nuclear weapons to the world. Within ten years other countries may have nuclear bombs, each of which, weighing less than a ton, could destroy an urban area of more than five square miles. In the war to which such an armaments race is likely to lead, the United States, with its agglomeration of population and industry in comparatively few metropolitan districts, will be at a disadvantage compared to the nations whose population and industry are scattered over large areas.

We believe that these considerations make the use of nuclear bombs for an early, unannounced attack against Japan inadvisable. If the United States would be the first to release this new means of indiscriminate destruction upon mankind, she would sacrifice public support throughout the world, precipitate the race for armaments, and prejudice the possibility of reaching an international agreement on the future control of such weapons.

Much more favorable conditions for the eventual achievement of such an agreement could be created if nuclear bombs were first revealed to the world by a demonstration in an appropriately selected uninhabited area.

If chances for the establishment of an effective international control of nuclear weapons will have to be considered slight at the present time, then not only the use of these weapons against Japan, but even their early demonstration may be contrary to the interests of this country. A postponement of such a demonstration will have in this case the advantage of delaying the beginning of the nuclear armaments race as long as possible. If, during the time gained, ample support could be made available for further development of the field in this country, the postponement would substantially increase the lead which we have established during the present war, and our position in an armament race or in any later attempt at international agreement will thus be strengthened.

On the other hand, if no adequate public support for the development of nucleonics will be available without a demonstration, the postponement of the latter may be deemed inadvisable, because enough information might leak out to cause other nations to start the armament race, in which we will then be at a disadvantage. At the same time, the distrust of other nations may be aroused by a confirmed development under cover of secrecy, making it more difficult eventually to reach an agreement with them.

If the government should decide in favor of an early demonstration of nuclear weapons it will then have the possibility to take into account the public opinion of this country and of the other nations before deciding whether these weapons should be used in the war against Japan. In this way, other nations may assume a share of the responsibility for such a fateful decision.

To sum up, we urge that the use of nuclear bombs in this war be considered as a problem of long-range national policy rather than military expediency, and that this policy be directed primarily to the achievement of an agreement permitting an effective international control of the means of nuclear warfare.

The vital importance of such a control for our country is obvious from the fact that the only effective alternative method of protecting this country, of which we are aware, would be a dispersal of our major cities and essential industries.

Scientists Urge the United States to Use the Bomb Immediately

In the following document, a group of scientists makes exactly the opposite recommendation as had the scientists who wrote the Franck report. Scientists who urge immediate use of the weapon believe that such use will contribute substantially to the war effort and that Japan will more likely surrender if the bomb is actually used. They consider the possibility, urged by others as a better first step, of demonstrating the destructiveness of atomic weapons to a select group of witnesses without actually using the bomb as a weapon. These scientists, however, do not believe such a demonstration would be sufficiently persuasive to Japan. In addition, they are aware of the likelihood of an invasion of Japan if the bomb is not used, and of the certainty of substantial American deaths during such an invasion. Their primary obligation, they believe, is to consider how the war could be ended more quickly, and how it could be ended with the fewest American casualties. Nevertheless, they do not recommend that the United States proceed against Japan in absolute isolation, but rather that the United States inform its allies of general "progress" made in the development of atomic weapons without explicitly stating that the United States is actually prepared to use the bomb. They conclude by acknowledging that the use of atomic power, for military or other purposes, will inevitably create new problems even as it appears to solve others.

FROM A. H. COMPTON, E. O. LAWRENCE, J. R. OPPENHEIMER, AND E. FERMI, "RECOMMENDATIONS ON THE IMMEDIATE USE OF NUCLEAR WEAPONS," JUNE 16, 1945

(U.S. National Archives, Record Group 77, Records of the Office of the Chief of Engineers, Manhattan Engineer District, Harrison-Bundy File, Folder 76)

You have asked us to comment on the initial use of the new weapon. This use, in our opinion, should be such as to promote a satisfactory adjustment of our international relations. At the same time, we recognize our obligation to our nation to use the weapon to help save American lives in the Japanese war.

(1) To accomplish these ends we recommend that before the weapons are used not only Britain, but also Russia, France, and China be advised that we have made considerable progress in our work on atomic weapons, that these may be ready to use during the present war, and that we would welcome suggestions as to how we can cooperate in making this development contribute to improved international relations.

(2) The opinions of our scientific colleagues on the initial use of these weapons are not unanimous: they range from the proposal of a purely technical demonstration to that of the military application best designed to induce surrender. Those who advocate a purely technical demonstration would wish to outlaw the use of atomic weapons, and have feared that if we use the weapons now our position in future negotiations will be prejudiced. Others emphasize the opportunity of saving American lives by immediate military use, and believe that such use will improve the international prospects, in that they are more concerned with the prevention of war than with the elimination of this specific weapon. We find ourselves closer to these latter views; we can propose no technical demonstration likely to bring an end to the war; we see no acceptable alternative to direct military use.

(3) With regard to these general aspects of the use of atomic energy, it is clear that we, as scientific men, have no proprietary rights. It is true that we are among the few citizens who have had occasion to give thoughtful consideration to these problems during the past few years. We have, however, no claim to special competence in solving the political, social, and military problems which are presented by the advent of atomic power.

NATIVE AMERICAN CONTRIBUTIONS TO THE WAR EFFORT: NAVAJO CODE TALKERS

Among the most famous Native American contributions to the war effort were the Navajo Code Talkers. This code would prove especially effective because so few people who were not Navajo spoke the Navajo language. Even if a person understood what the code talkers were saying in Navajo, however, that person would still not be able to break the code without understanding how the Navajo words were being used. The alphabetic portion of the code is reproduced below. When speaking in code, a Navajo would essentially spell out every word, rather than simply say the word, with the additional step of translating everything from English into Navajo. Every letter of the English alphabet was assigned an English word, and that word was translated into Navajo. For example, if a person wanted to use the word "island," he would first identify the English words affiliated with the letters in "island": ice, sheep, lamb, ant, nut, deer. Then he would translate those words into Navajo, so in order to communicate "island," the speaker would have to say, "tkin, dibeh, dibeh-yazzie, wol-la-chee, nesh-chee, be." Obviously, even a short sentence would take considerably longer to say in this code.

FROM "NAVAJO CODE"

(National Archives and Records Administration, Part 1; Folder 6, Box 5; History and Museums Division; Records Relating to Public Affairs; USMC Reserve and Historical Studies, 1942–1988)

English Letter	Navaho Word	Meaning
A	Wol-la-chee	Ant
B	Shush	Bear
C	Moasi	Cat
D	Be	Deer
E	Czeh	Elk
F	Ma-e	Fox
G	Klizzie	Goat
H	Lin	Horse
I	Tkin	Ice
J	Tkele-cho-gi	Jackass
K	Klizzie-yazzie	Kid
L	Dibeh-yazzie	Lamb

M	Na-as-tso-si	Mouse
N	Nesh-chee	Nut
O	Ne-ahs-jah	Owl
P	Bi-so-dih	Pig
Q	Ca-yeilth	Quiver
R	Cah	Rabbit
S	Dibeh	Sheep
T	Than-zie	Turkey
U	No-da-ih	Ute
V	A-keh-di-glini	Victor
W	Gloe-ih	Weasel
X	Al-an-as-dzoh	Cross
Y	Tsah-as-zih	Yucca
Z	Besh-do-gliz	Zinc

TOPICS FOR WRITTEN OR ORAL EXPLORATION

1. Discuss the extent to which Tayo's condition in the novel is a result of his wartime experiences. What other factors contribute to his situation?

2. Examine the scene during which Tayo enlists in the military. What are his motives? To what extent does he feel ambivalent? Compare Tayo's goals in making his decision with the goals of men and women who join the military today.

3. Analyze Tayo's description of the landscape of the Philippines. Compare the geography and climate of the Philippines to the geography and climate of New Mexico. What factors contribute to Tayo's physical discomfort when he is away from home?

4. Write an essay in which you discuss how you came to make a difficult decision, especially a decision about which you felt ambivalent. Were any particular individuals especially influential as you made your decision?

5. Compare President Roosevelt's speech included above to the speeches of other world leaders, such as Churchill or Hitler, during World War II, or compare Roosevelt's speech to speeches delivered by other American presidents during times of war.

6. Write a speech in which you attempt to persuade a broad audience, such as an entire nation, to unite in the face of a difficult situation, such as a military attack, an economic depression, or another national emergency.

7. Examine several newspaper or magazine articles reporting the events of World War II or another war. To what extent is the reporting objective? Where do you detect bias?

8. Interview a veteran of World War II or any subsequent war. To what extent were his or her experiences similar to or different from those of Art Shedd or the veterans in *Ceremony*?

9. Compare American responses to foreign attacks (e.g., Pearl Harbor, the World Trade Center) and to domestic attacks (e.g., the Oklahoma City bombing, the sniper attacks in Virginia during 2003). Does the source of an attack affect the public's reaction?

10. Research the participation of members of your own ethnic group during World War II or another war.

11. Research the American government's treatment of its citizens or residents who share ethnicity with enemies of the United States during a war, for example Japanese or Germans during World War II, Arab Americans during the Gulf Wars.

12. Organize a debate in your class regarding the use of the atomic bomb. Was its use justified during World War II? How should atomic weapons be regulated today?

13. Watch a movie about World War II and discuss whether the thematic issues and attitudes toward the war resemble those presented in *Ceremony*. Examples include *Patton*, *Dr. Strangelove*, *The Sands of Iwo Jima*, and *Pearl Harbor*.

14. Read another novel that includes a character or characters who are veterans. How do their experiences compare to Tayo's? Examples include *The Things They Carried*

by Tim O'Brien, *A Farewell to Arms* by Ernest Hemingway, *Cold Mountain* by Charles Frazier, and *Red Earth: A Vietnam Warrior's Journey* by Philip Red Eagle.

15. Write a few sentences in Navajo Code and have a classmate translate it back into English. How long does the translation take? Discuss the advantages and disadvantages of such a code.

16. Research code-making and code-breaking. What are the features that make a code particularly difficult to break? What strategies do intelligence officers use in attempting to break codes? Try to create an "unbreakable" code of your own.

SUGGESTED READING

Bataan Rescue: The Most Daring Rescue of World War II. Dir. Peter Jones. The American Experience, WGBH Boston, 2003.

Bernstein, Alison R. *American Indians and World War II: Toward a New Era in Indian Affairs.* Norman: University of Oklahoma Press, 1991.

Chang, Iris. *The Rape of Nanking: The Forgotten Holocaust of World War II.* New York: Basic Books, 1997.

Donovan, R. J. *P.T.-109: John F. Kennedy in World War 2.* New York: McGraw-Hill, 1961.

Franco, Jere Bishop. *Crossing the Pond: The Native American Effort in World War II.* Denton: University of North Texas Press, 1999.

Hemingway, Albert. *Ira Hayes, Pima Marine.* Lanham, MD: University Press of America, 1988.

Hersey, John. *Hiroshima.* New York: Bantam Books, 1948.

Hynes, Samuel, et al., eds. *Reporting World War II: American Journalism 1938–1946.* 2 vols. New York: Library of America, 1995.

Lee, Clark. *They Call It Pacific: An Eye-Witness Story of Our War Against Japan from Bataan to the Solomons.* New York: Viking Press, 1943.

Norton, Donald J., and Charles E. Yeager. *Chippewa Chief in World War II: The Survival Story of Oliver Rasmussen in Japan.* Jefferson, NC: McFarland and Co., 2001.

Townsend, William, and Constance Little. *World War II and the American Indian.* Albuquerque: University of New Mexico Press, 2002.

Walker, J. Samuel. *Prompt and Utter Destruction: Truman and the Use of Atomic Bombs Against Japan.* Chapel Hill: University of North Carolina Press, 1997.

4

Traditional Native American Spirituality and Western Medicine

CEREMONY, ILLNESS, AND SPIRITUALITY

When *Ceremony* opens, Tayo is returning to Laguna after serving in the army during World War II and after being discharged from a military psychiatric hospital. His illness, diagnosed by military personnel as battle fatigue, has a number of causes, not all of which are directly related to the war. Although Tayo is not fully—or even substantially—cured, the hospital has discharged him because the doctors there do not believe additional treatment will prove fruitful. At best, they hope that relocating Tayo to a more familiar and familial environment will encourage his recovery. Nevertheless, the doctors also disparage traditional medicine, assuming that if science can't cure him, nothing else can either.

A conflict between a Western scientific view of the world with the interpretive strategies particular to that view and a traditional Native American view with other interpretive strategies emerges frequently in the novel. Although this conflict is not the most prominent one in the book, it affects a number of others. Characters such as Rocky will be drawn toward the authoritative influence of science and the power it represents, while other characters will be repelled by it. Part of Tayo's task in the novel is to understand his own position within this argument.

The Western scientific view assumes that knowledge can be divided into disciplinary categories—there's biology, physics, history, literature, and so forth—and that the knowledge contained in one discipline is different from the knowledge contained in another. Theology is not biology, nor is horticul-

ture mathematics. These disciplinary boundaries extend into the professions—
a priest is not generally a doctor, and if he is, he has earned credentials beyond
those required for a priest; a degree from a divinity school does not grant one
a license to practice medicine. To people raised within the Western worldview,
this all makes perfect sense; it's absolutely logical. In addition to categorizing
knowledge this way, the West also prioritizes certain kinds of knowledge above
others. Currently, scientific knowledge—in part because it has led to such dra-
matic technological changes, but also because flawed scientific ideas can sometimes be disproved comparatively easily—holds more authority than other
types of knowledge. The scientific method relies on empirical evidence, that
which can be seen and measured. And Western ideas of evidence assume that
written texts are more reliable than memories conveyed orally. Other cultural
views, including the tradition of Laguna Pueblo, would dispute the division
of knowledge this way and challenge the worth and effectiveness of a practice
that does not strive for the integration of various types of knowledge. The
Pueblo people also observe their world, of course, but their interpretations of
those observations differ sharply from a conventional scientist's.

In *Ceremony,* these cultural differences are most prominently illustrated when
Josiah is trying to decide which variety of cattle would be best suited to the dry
environment of New Mexico. According to many scientists, Herefords make an
ideal breed; they're stocky enough to provide sufficient beef to compensate for
a farmer's investment. The scientists who recommend short, stocky cattle, however, assume that the only priority is the farmer's financial gain, and that one
farmer is interchangeable with another. Reading material he's received from the
agricultural extension agent, Josiah is puzzled because the books make recommendations that seem senseless to him. He wonders whether he has misunder-
stood the authors, but Rocky and Tayo confirm his interpretation. Josiah's goal
is to acquire cattle capable of surviving harsh droughts and poor vegetation, cattle characterized by a bit of a wild streak, cattle as vigorous as the land is severe.
Herefords, Josiah believes, would die of thirst before they would walk half a mile
to water. The scientists have failed to adjust their recommendations to account
for different environments; to Josiah, his specific environment must be considered first. Josiah decides to buy the Mexican cattle, although they resemble deer
as much as they resemble Herefords. When Tayo sees them for the first time, he
thinks of the "diagram of the ideal beef cow which had been in the back of one
of his books, and these cattle were everything that the ideal cow was not" (75).

Rocky, on the other hand, is skeptical. He urges Josiah to pay attention to
the books, to adhere to the recommendations of the scientists. Books possess
an authority that personal experience, even extensive personal experience, never
will. Even the word "scientist," anonymous as it is, evokes a respect that the
term "Uncle Josiah" never will. Scientists, Rocky claims, "know everything

there is to know about beef cattle" (76). Obviously, Rocky gives scientists more credit than they deserve; the important point, however, is not whether scientists do "know everything," but that Rocky and others like him believe scientists do. Rocky speaks with authority because they're discussing "books and scientific knowledge—those things that Rocky had learned to believe in" (76). Scientists, in other words, don't represent truth but a belief system. And the scientific belief system demands that other belief systems be rejected. Rocky can't respect science and also adhere to traditional spiritual practices; rather, he must declare those practices to be superstition.

Tayo remembers an incident when he and Rocky had been out hunting. Like most of his relatives, Tayo practices certain rituals as the deer is slain, but Rocky refuses to. When Josiah and Robert arrive, they "sprinkled cornmeal on the nose and fed the deer's spirit. They had to show their love and respect, their appreciation; otherwise, the deer would be offended, and they would not come to die for them the following year" (51). Rocky feels embarrassed for the others and for himself since he is associated with them. The ritual continues after they bring the deer home, but "Rocky tried to tell them that keeping the carcass on the floor in a warm room was bad for the meat. He wanted to hang the deer in the woodshed, where the meat would stay cold and cure properly" (52). Perhaps sprinkling cornmeal at the snout of a slain animal is superstitious; perhaps human survival in a hunting culture has nothing to do with this ritual. Nevertheless, the ritual demonstrates a respect for other living creatures and a humility regarding the role of humanity in the universe that Rocky's utilitarian attitude abandons. The ritual, in other words, isn't performed for itself alone, but for the attitude it expresses. By rejecting the ritual, Rocky also denies the value of his family's culture's attitude.

The physicians employed by the military also insist that Tayo reject his cultural practices. In response to Old Grandma's insistence that Tayo needs a medicine man, Auntie responds that the doctor had warned them, "No Indian medicine" (34). When he had been in the hospital, Tayo had felt as if he existed without substance, as if he were simply shadow or smoke. He had been prescribed medicine that affected his memory; perhaps it also decreased his agitation, but Tayo's cure will eventually occur with the reconciliation of his memory with his present life, a reconciliation that is impossible as long as he is medicated in this way. Although one doctor seems sympathetic to Tayo's condition and discharges him with the belief that he's more likely to achieve a cure in a familiar and presumably more comfortable setting, the system of treatment itself inhibits Tayo's cure; it even permits Tayo to avoid a cure by permitting him to remain insubstantial. After Tayo arrives home, in fact, he longs to return to the hospital so that he can become inanimate, so that he can disappear into the objects around him.

The doctors had explained to Auntie and Robert that battle fatigue, as Tayo's condition is described, is so difficult to treat, in part, because its causes are so unclear. Readers of *Ceremony*, however, can point to at least three contributing factors in Tayo's specific case. Despite orders to do so, he is unable to shoot the Japanese soldiers because he believes at least one is Uncle Josiah; he believes, in other words, that he is killing a relative rather than an enemy. Subsequently, he witnesses a Japanese soldier jab his rifle butt into Rocky's skull. Tayo believes that Rocky should have returned home and that he, Tayo, has returned only because the military has somehow mistakenly forgotten to bury his corpse. Tayo believes he's dead, in other words, but not buried. In addition, because of the conditions on the march, Tayo has cursed both the rain and the flies, although he has been taught to honor both. He believes his curses, which he can't revoke, have created the drought that Laguna is currently experiencing. Tayo's condition, however, also has causes that extend beyond his military experiences, and the ceremony that cures him will incorporate aspects of those other causes.

Although Tayo is the only significant character in *Ceremony* who is described as suffering from battle fatigue, he is by no means the only soldier who suffers negative effects from the demands of war. Harley's emotions seem to have been completely repressed. He banters his way through situations, but he doesn't feel an actual response to any given situation. Superficially, he appears to function much more normally than Tayo does—Harley doesn't lie in bed all day vomiting when light filters through the shade, for example. Yet Harley seems to exist on a purely physical plane—his emotional life and his spiritual life are dead. He is not that different from Tayo, therefore, who claims to be a walking corpse. Emo, too, has absorbed his war experiences and converted them almost into an addiction; he thrives on violence—violence feeds his spirit. The type of evil Emo represents, however, is much more insidious than the result of a single war. The war may have functioned as the catalyst for Emo's lust for violence, but had the war not occurred, some other experience likely would have filled this role. While Harley fails to resist the witchery, Emo actively cultivates it.

The ceremony that Old Betonie describes to Tayo—and essentially prescribes for him—addresses the level of violence in the world, as it also addresses the numerous factors that have led to Tayo's condition. By completing this ceremony, Tayo achieves a fuller understanding not only of the nature of the world but also of his own identity. Paradoxically, he must also integrate his identity in order to complete the ceremony properly and reject the temptations of witchery.

Although the entire novel is itself ceremonial, beginning and ending with chants that honor the sunrise, Tayo's particular ceremony begins most unequivocally with his visit to Old Betonie. Like Tayo, Old Betonie has mixed-race ancestry, and he seems an unlikely wisdom figure, living as he does in the foothills outside Gallup, surrounded by piles of newspapers, calendars, and telephone books. Like the psychiatrist, Old Betonie asks Tayo to speak, but unlike the psychiatrist who has been trained not to disclose details of his personal life to his patients, Old Betonie also tells his own story to Tayo. Old Betonie will recognize Tayo's cure by listening to his story and recognizing the mythic details it contains. Tayo's story is part of a greater story, and to find his way back to himself, Tayo must learn how to identify his position within the story.

After introducing his assistant, Shush, implicitly a bear-child, Old Betonie recites a chant about a man who has been stolen by Coyote, the Trickster figure. The man's relatives consult the Bear People, who have "power to restore the mind" (141). The Bear People offer a series of instructions, concluding with the necessity of creating a Pollen Boy. When the chant ends, Tayo is sitting in a sand painting that matches the details of the chant. To the extent that the ceremony will have curative power, Tayo's mind has already begun to be healed. In the way of many prophets, Old Betonie doesn't explicitly instruct Tayo in the course he must follow but rather describes the signs he must recognize, including a pattern of stars in the sky that Tayo will use to locate Uncle Josiah's stolen cattle. Old Betonie also clarifies that Tayo's vision of Uncle Josiah among the Japanese soldiers is not entirely illogical since Asians and Native Americans are distant relatives. To complete his ceremony, Tayo must fulfill his promise to help Josiah with the cattle, and he must accept his role in the universal battle against witchery. Several of his encounters—with the woman called T'seh for example—as he enacts Old Betonie's prophecy have a mystical or supernatural element, as if Tayo's actions will have a more profound effect on the world than would be expected.

Tayo's greatest temptation occurs when he witnesses Emo and Pinkie torturing Harley, and he imagines jamming a screwdriver into Emo's skull. Although he might save Harley by killing Emo, Tayo recognizes that participating in such violence would have the effect of aligning himself with the witchery. In order to overcome the evil released and spread through witchery, Tayo must resist evil acts, even when they seem justified. The novel implies that had Tayo surrendered to his temptation, the world might not have survived. Tayo's responsibility is to a much greater cosmic force than his own individual psychic discomfort.

The final stage of Tayo's ceremony occurs when he enters a kiva with Ku'oosh and other members of the medicine society. As Tayo tells his story, the other men ask him repeatedly about Night Swan. Because she has appeared to Tayo, the people will be blessed. Because Tayo has completed the ceremony, the world has been granted, at least for a time, a stay against destruction. And Tayo, too, is cured; the man who was stolen by Coyote is relieved of his coyote skin and of the evil it embodied. Tayo's cure is effected, in other words, not because his individual self is treated, but rather through his recognition of his connection to time, to place, and to other human and nonhuman creatures.

BATTLE FATIGUE

Tayo's condition is defined by his military physicians as "battle fatigue," a term that was used during and after World War II regarding soldiers who suffered from certain psychological conditions as a result of their military experience. Prior to World War II, doctors documented other types of mental illness in the military, especially during war. Until the twentieth century, however, these cases were comparatively uncommon. During World War I, the number of soldiers treated for and discharged because of mental illnesses increased substantially. At that time, the condition was referred to as "shell shock," originally because physicians believed that the soldiers had suffered brain injuries as a result of nearby exploding bombs. Doctors eventually rejected that theory and defined the condition as psychological rather than biological. Nevertheless, current theories that attempt to explain the increase in psychological illnesses as a result of twentieth-century wars do point to changes in military technology—the increased destructiveness of weapons, for example, that soldiers would be required to witness—as one cause.

Because of its inaccuracy, the term "shell shock" was rejected by the time World War II began, and soldiers suffering similar symptoms were diagnosed with battle fatigue. Currently, psychologists and psychiatrists prefer to call the condition post-traumatic stress disorder. Although post-traumatic stress can affect individuals who have not participated in war (e.g., those who are victims of or witnesses to other types of violence), soldiers are at a particularly high risk due to the inevitable trauma and stress of war.

Psychiatric and other illnesses were particularly prevalent in the Pacific— more than in European theaters of the war. In general, Pacific conditions were dramatically different than European conditions. Allied soldiers frequently had to cut their way through the jungle, for example, before engaging in a battle against the Japanese. No infrastructure, such as roads and fresh water supplies, existed to transport or support troops. Buildings that could be converted into hospitals did not exist, so doctors performed their duties in temporary facilities until hospitals could be erected. The situation was exacerbated by the prevalence of diseases uncommon in Europe or the United States, such as malaria, to which all soldiers in the Philippines were exposed. For much of the war, some hospitals in the southwest portion of the Pacific lacked psychiatrists entirely, and even after the war in Europe ended, psychiatric services in the Pacific region were insufficient, not only because of the lack of personnel, but also because of the lack of equipment and appropriate medication. As a result, the conditions of many soldiers were misdiagnosed for several days or even weeks until a psychiatrist could be consulted.

When a soldier was hospitalized for psychiatric reasons, his prognosis often depended on who treated him. Many commanding officers deemed such soldiers as completely useless and suggested they be immediately discharged. (These officers often assumed that recruitment officers should have detected the psychiatric condition and rejected the recruit.) Such a practice, however, resulted in such a substantial loss of personnel that the military would have been unable to maintain a sufficient force in the Pacific had these discharges continued throughout the war. Psychiatrists themselves argued that with appropriate treatment, many, even most, psychiatric patients could return to active duty. In some hospitals, as many as 50 percent of the patients were treated effectively enough so that they could return to battle. Others would be reassigned to support services. If a soldier could not return to duty, often because of more serious psychotic conditions, he would be returned to the United States; such a trip took about 30 days by ship and was hence arduous both for him and for the personnel caring for him. By the end of the war, such patients were evacuated by plane; because the trip then took approximately 30 hours rather than 30 days, the patients could be heavily sedated for the entire journey.

Psychiatric treatment improved during the war. By 1944 many soldiers suffering from psychological conditions could be kept at battalion aid posts or evacuation hospitals for a few days of rest and sedation; they would then be able to return to duty. While at the hospital, a soldier might engage in occupational therapy, such as building furniture or constructing sports facilities, and in group therapy. Initially, many commanding officers, even those staffing hospitals, disparaged occupational therapy because some of the activities—knitting or needlepoint, for example—were stereotypically feminine and hence not manly enough for soldiers; when other activities such as radio repair or carpentry were added, those commanding officers often realized the therapy's value. When occupational therapy did not compose part of the program, patients often became so apathetic and bored that their conditions disintegrated further. Individual psychotherapy was used occasionally, but personnel were too limited to make this a common practice. Drugs, especially sedatives, were also used, but supplies of other psychiatric medications were limited—and medications available during the 1940s were not nearly as effective as those available today. Most psychiatrists would have preferred to use electroshock therapy—seldom used any longer—with their patients, but the equipment was unavailable in this region.

After the war, nearly all returning military personnel experienced some social, economic, or medical difficulties. The military offered some services as soldiers were discharged, translating, for example, specific military experiences into civilian job categories. Organizations in large cities also established centers where veterans could receive assistance with employment and health care. Many of these newly discharged men joined veterans' organizations, at least temporarily, for support and comradery as they became assimilated back into civilian life. Conversations when veterans socialized with each other generally consisted of war stories, similar to the stories Harley and Emo tell in an attempt to relive the excitement of the war. In addition, the United States Congress passed the G.I. Bill, which provided veterans with, among other things, assistance with higher education.

Because of stigmas associated with mental illness, soldiers who had been psychiatric patients often anticipated more problems readjusting to civilian life than soldiers who could return as unequivocal heroes. Nevertheless, nearly all of these veterans were able to find employment relatively quickly, although few of them were completely free of the symptoms of their illnesses. In the decade following the war, many received disability payments from the Veterans Administration, ranging from $1.00 to $189.00 per month. Most of these men, unfortunately, did not receive ongoing treatment, and many did not receive any medical treatment after they left the military. In addition, a small but significant group developed psychiatric conditions after they left the military, due in part to their experiences during the war.

ALTERNATIVE AND COMPLEMENTARY MEDICINE

Today, a sizable number, though probably not the majority, of Americans rely on a range of nontraditional medical practices instead of or in addition to seeing a conventional physician. Most of these treatments have not been scientifically proven to be effective, which is not to say that they've been proven ineffective, either, since many of them have not been tested according to scientific standards. They range from particular types of diets, perhaps with herbal and vitamin supplements, to practices such as acupuncture, aromatherapy, and meditation. A disadvantage of relying on practices that have not been tested is that while some may in fact be helpful, others may be worthless or even dangerous. Some people assume that any "natural" product must by definition be safe, but many toxic substances occur naturally in the environment. People who follow these regimens do so for a number of reasons, from disaffection with the conventional medical system that too often attends to the illness while ignoring the patient, to desperation when a conventional physician declares a condition terminal.

Because so many Americans—including some doctors—have become disillusioned with (or have begun to acknowledge the limitations of) standard medicine, some medical schools have begun offering instruction in other types of treatment, including some traditional Native American practices. Students enrolled in these courses would likely recommend these treatments as a supplement to rather than a substitute for conventional medicine. For example, few oncologists would suggest that meditation or massage cures cancer, yet they might agree that a relaxed and an optimistic patient will experience greater success with chemotherapy than will a depressed and tense patient. Most contemporary evidence suggests that there are numerous links between the mind and the body—if the two can actually be separated—but how those links work remains mysterious.

When someone is considering complementary or alternative medicines, that person should make every effort to gather reliable information about both the practice and the practitioner. (This advice is also true for conventional medicine but even more important for alternative practices, since they are less well-regulated.) Individuals who are taking dietary supplements or herbal medicines need to inform their primary care physicians, since some products affect the efficacy of prescription drugs. Because traditional insurance companies tend not to cover alternative practices, cost may also be a concern.

One alternative "treatment" linking spirituality and medicine that has recently garnered substantial attention is the power of prayer. To some religious people, especially Christians, praying for the health of oneself and others is a very typical practice; nonbelievers, however, have generally assumed that any cures attributed to prayer (or miracles) could be explained scientifically, if not now then at some point in the future when further scientific discoveries have been accomplished. Many (though not all) religions include some type of ceremony (often less elaborate than the ceremony Tayo completes) intended to induce healing. Some Christian denominations refer to this practice as the sacrament of the sick; others call it the laying on of hands. Regardless of the name applied, this practice always involves prayer within the context of ritual. In addition, many people pray privately, asking for benefits for themselves or others from God. Skeptics, however, could argue that cures occur not because prayer is effective but rather because the patient believes that the prayer will work; prayer is simply a placebo. If prayer actually helps cure illness, then it should work whether or not the patient believes in the prayer or even knows that he or she is being prayed for.

To test this idea, some doctors have studied the effect of prayer on their patients. A flurry of newspaper and magazine articles appeared following a study by Dr. Rogerio A. Lobo, a physician teaching at the Columbia University School of Medicine, and another by Dr. Mitchell W. Krucoff, a physician teaching at Duke University Medical Center. Dr. Lobo's patients were women living in Korea and experiencing problems with fertility. Prayer groups in Canada, Australia, and the United States prayed for some of the women but not others; the women did not know they were being prayed for, nor did the medical personnel who were caring for them. Compared to the women who were not prayed for, twice as many women who were prayed for became pregnant. Dr. Krucoff is a cardiologist, and his patients were undergoing angioplasty. Again, some patients were prayed for, while others were not. The ones who were prayed for experienced fewer complications during surgery than those who were not. A similar study of heart patients was conducted by Dr. Randolph C. Byrd during the 1980s, and his patients experienced similar results. Many people were, of course, surprised by the outcome of these studies.

To date, several hundred studies have been completed asking similar questions; because many of them have failed to establish a relationship between prayer and recovery, the scientific community has not yet reached a consensus on this issue. These studies are also difficult to conduct according to scientific standards, since patients are often prayed for by family members and friends who are not participating in the experiment; a control group consisting of patients who are absolutely not prayed for by anyone is virtually impossible to establish.

NATIVE AMERICAN CEREMONIALISM

Although most Native American tribes have historically organized themselves around the roles various individuals may play, those roles are not distinguished in the same way that other Americans delineate professional responsibilities. For example, the roles of priest, doctor, and political leader are not absolutely distinct in Native American cultures, as they are to the majority of other Americans. And as we have seen, much of Native American life is accompanied by ceremony, so that activities like planting, harvesting, hunting, and childbearing involve ritual. The antonyms "secular" and "religious" don't carry the weight in Native American cultures that they do in mainstream American culture.

Pueblo ceremonies (and most Native American traditions) generally integrate natural elements into the ritual. Corn pollen is one of the most common substances used, reflecting the culture's reliance on corn for its survival. Corn pollen serves to bless both people and animals and also to illustrate the event that a given ceremony recalls and reenacts. Most rituals, one must remember, aren't simply performances like plays or movies; instead, rituals collapse time between the original event and the present so that the event is literally happening again. Belief in ritual implies belief in a cyclic rather than exclusively linear concept of time. For example, one of the poems in *Ceremony* describes a time when a boy became a bear; after he returns to his human form, he still retains bear-like qualities. The story isn't simply a fairy tale of an imagined event that might have occurred long, long ago; instead, it is intended, in part, to explain events that continue to happen in the present. Children still get captured by animals or animal spirits, and Old Betonie's assistant is such a child.

Some Native American ceremonies occur on feast days. Through syncretism, these feast days have become linked to the Christian calendar. Laguna Pueblo celebrations that are open to the public include the Feasts of St. Joseph on March 19, which includes a harvest dance, and on September 19, which includes buffalo, corn, and eagle dances. Harvest dances are also performed at Laguna on July 26, the feast day of St. Ann, and on September 8, the Nativity, or birthday, of the Virgin Mary, as well as on September 25, the feast day of St. Elizabeth, and on various other days. Other pueblos pay particular attention to other Christian saints, and many pueblos celebrate significant holidays like Easter and Christmas with dances. These associations between Native American traditions and Christian holy days occur as a result of the strong missionary presence in the Southwest centuries ago. The missionary church at Laguna Pueblo was originally dedicated to St. Joseph, which is why Laguna pays particular attention to him.

The following documents explore the relationships between Native American healing practices and conventional Western medicine, especially psychiatry. The first document is a myth that reveals the origin of the Medicine Man. Next is a table relating health statistics of veterans of World War II. Following that, two documents describe psychiatric interpretations of battle fatigue and post-traumatic stress disorder. Then come three descriptions of additional healing ceremonies in the Pueblo tradition, followed by two excerpts comparing the training and practices of Native American healers with conventional physicians. Finally, an editorial examines the public response to the suggestion that Christian prayer has actual healing power.

ORIGIN MYTH OF THE MEDICINE MAN

The following excerpt describes how the identity of a medicine man came to be. Through supernatural means, the people had become sick, and they could not treat their illness through ordinary means. As is true in many polytheistic cultures, one god is sometimes able to counteract or moderate the actions of another. Iatiku does not cure the people directly but provides them the means for a cure. Because of the success of the original medicine man, additional clans establish medicine societies. Notice that bears are said to have the power to cure illnesses caused by witches, that is, by evil actions or desires, illnesses that would include Tayo's. Notice, also, the significance of the number four in this ceremony.

FROM RAMÓN A. GUTIÉRREZ, *WHEN JESUS CAME, THE CORN MOTHERS WENT AWAY*

(Stanford University Press, 1991)

The people had never known sickness until the serpent Pishuni returned as a plague. The people tried to cure themselves, but could not. To break Pishuni's spell Iatiku created the *chaianyi,* the Medicine Man. The oldest man of the Oak clan was made Fire Medicine Man because fire was the strongest thing that Sun had given them and oak burned hottest. Corn Mother told Oak Man to go to North Mountain and there in a pine tree that had been struck by lightning he would find an obsidian arrowhead that would be his heart and his protection. She taught him how to make black prayer sticks as symbols of the night in which he would work, and then made him an altar. Iatiku taught the Medicine Man how to mix medicines and how to secure the power of bears to destroy disease-causing witches. "Now I will make you *honani* [corn fetish] so that you will remember me," Iatiku said to the chaianyi, "it will have my power." Into a corn cob she blew her breath along with a few drops of honey to symbolize all plant food. The cob was wrapped in four husks and dressed with the tail feather of a roadrunner and of a magpie to make it useful in prayers. Iatiku also placed turquoise on the corn fetish so that it would always have the power to make one attractive and loved.

Everything was ready for a cure so Iatiku said to Fire Medicine Man, "Let us try it out." For four days the medicine man did not touch women, salt, or meat, and only sang and prayed. On the fourth night he performed a cure. The people quickly recovered. When Iatiku saw this, she also created the Flint, Spider, and Giant Medicine Societies. (6)

WESTERN MEDICINE AND PSYCHIATRY

The next three documents look specifically at how conventional Western medicine responds to injuries suffered and conditions experienced as a result of war. First, a chart reveals the types of illnesses reported by veterans of World War II in the six years immediately following the war. Then, a longer document written by a man who was a general and chief surgeon during the war speaks very critically of soldiers who experience battle fatigue. His attitude was not uncommon at the time—which is one reason why successful psychiatric facilities were so difficult to establish near the front lines—though many of his suggestions seem particularly harsh now. His memorandum is followed by an excerpt from a contemporary psychiatric manual, including the requirements for a diagnosis of post-traumatic stress disorder. The manual is intended to be more objective than the memorandum; yet, even so, one can see the attitudinal shift regarding mental illness that occurred during the second half of the twentieth century.

Veterans' Postwar Medical Conditions

The following chart lists the rate of illness among four groups of World War II veterans: those who were prisoners of war in the Pacific (PWJ), a control group of those who fought in the Pacific (WJ), those who were prisoners of war in Europe (PWE), and a control group of those who fought in Europe (WE). In almost every case, soldiers who had been held prisoners of war by the Japanese experienced a higher incidence of illness, sometimes significantly so. Although the number of men studied in each category is similar, veterans who had been prisoners of the Japanese not only suffered higher rates of many illnesses, but they also suffered a greater number of separate illnesses. Tayo's experience, therefore, would have been among the harshest suffered by American soldiers, and his condition following the war would have been far from unique. Several factors account for these differences. Because Japan was not a signatory to the Geneva Convention treaties regarding the treatment of prisoners of war, Japan was not legally obligated to provide the same level of care to its prisoners as was Germany. Many of the illnesses listed below—even if they are not caused by malnutrition—can be exacerbated by poor nutrition and sanitation. Because the average stay in a Japanese prisoner of war camp was significantly longer than in a European one, malnutrition became more profound for Japanese prisoners. In addition, some types of illness occur more frequently in hot, humid climates, such as is found in the Philippines, than in more northern climates. Notice, for example, how comparatively uncommon malaria is in veterans who were stationed in Europe. These factors could compound any predisposition to mental illness; over twice as many Pacific veterans sought help for psychiatric conditions as did European veterans.

FROM BERNARD M. COHEN AND MAURICE Z. COOPER, *A FOLLOW-UP STUDY OF WORLD WAR II PRISONERS OF WAR*

(Veterans Administration and the National Research Council, U.S. Government Printing Office, 1954)

From Disease and Impairment Categories in Which Hospital Diagnoses Received After Liberation Are Classified, and Number of Men in Each Category, by Roster

Diagnostic category	PWJ	WJ	PWE	WE
Tuberculosis, all forms	18	4	3	...
Syphilis	14	...	3	5
Venereal disease (VD) other than syphilis	11	3	3	4
Dysentery	42	2	1	...
Malaria	21	27	...	6
Helminthous disease	151	1	...	...
Other infective and parasitic diseases	49	13	22	15
Neoplasm, malignant	3	1	1	...
Neoplasm, benign and unspecified	12	1	4	2
Beriberi	40	...	...	...
Malnutrition, unspecified	296	1	44	...
Other nutritional deficiency	18	...	2	...
Eye condition, due to nutritional deficiency	15	...	...	...
Psychosis	11	10	3	4
Psychoneurosis, and other NP [neuropsychotic] condition	75	14	33	8
Refractive error of eye	34	1	2	...
Other eye condition, not due to nutritional deficiency	16	3	8	3
Deafness	15	1	1	1
Other ear condition	16	5	3	1
Rheumatic fever, heart disease, hypertension, and arteriosclerosis	20	4	4	1

Varicose veins	21	5	6	5
Other disease of arteries and veins, and disease of lymphatic system	6	1	2	…
Pneumonia	7	4	3	1
Other respiratory diseases	85	27	39	26
Diseases of oral cavity	30	4	7	3
Peptic ulcer	7	3	5	1
Gastritis, enteritis, and functional intestinal disorders	28	4	23	1
Hernia	15	2	3	4
Diseases of liver, gallbladder, and pancreas	6	2	1	…
Gastrointestinal symptoms	4	1	1	1
Other diseases of digestive system	14	4	3	2
Genitourinary diseases, non-VD	32	7	9	14
Diseases of skin and cellular tissue	66	16	22	18
Diseases of bones and organs of movement	42	10	16	8
Wounds or injuries, including residuals, and treatment for	97	21	73	23
Other conditions	81	7	23	11
Total number of categories	1,418	209	373	168
Number of men	492	521	462	461
Number of categories per man	2.88	0.40	0.81	0.36

The Chief Surgeon's Recommendations Regarding Battle Fatigue

The following memorandum illustrates a view of mental illness that was common in the mid-twentieth century and that continues to exist today, though to a lesser extent. Major General Hawley states unequivocally that the primary cause of battle fatigue—and implicitly some other psychological conditions—lies within the soldier. He lacks courage. He can succeed in life only if his stress is sufficiently minimal. Although *Ceremony* doesn't include any substantial scenes including Tayo's superior officers, some of the characters at Laguna exhibit similar, if less extreme, views as Major General Hawley. To a lesser extent, Hawley blames poor leadership. The weak soldier has no one to whom he can look to model appropriate courage. Although Hawley acknowledges that everyone has a breaking point, his attitude is entirely unsympathetic, as evidenced by his vocabulary: soldiers "malinger"; they are "weaklings" and "worthless" and "poor material." He also discounts the condition by describing the causes as "irritants." Hawley's solution is drastic. He suggests that the military cure soldiers' fear of the enemy by making them more afraid of their commanding officers. Any soldier who collapses from fear of the enemy should be executed. Hawley argues that fear of certain death, regardless of its source, will be more powerful than fear of possible death. Although he likely realized that his suggestion would not be implemented, his willingness to state it so bluntly in an official document indicates that he authentically believed in its potential efficacy. His suggestion is serious, in other words, not ironic.

FROM LEONARD D. HEATON AND ROBERT S. ANDERSON ET AL., *NEUROPSYCHIATRY IN WORLD WAR II,* VOL. II, *OVERSEAS THEATERS*

(Office of the Surgeon General, Department of the Army, 1973), Leonard D. Heaton, Robert S. Anderson, et al.

Memorandum—Psychoneurosis (Combat Exhaustion)

Headquarters
Communications Zone
European Theater of Operations
United States Army
APO 887
Office of the Chief Surgeon
4 August 1944

1. *Definition* Psychoneurosis is a *condition,* not a disease, which results from an individual surrendering to an adverse situation. It manifests itself in many ways and in varying degrees from a mild hypochondria to a severe anxiety neurosis.

2. *Cause*

   a. *General: The basic cause of psychoneurosis is insufficient courage* Courage is not to be confused with bravery. A courageous man may be badly frightened, but does not surrender to his fright. The amount of courage required by an individual to cope successfully with his environment is in inverse proportion to the friendliness of his environment. A man almost devoid of courage is able to lead a life of some usefulness so long as he is spared the necessity of confronting hostile or troublesome situations.

   b. *Psychoneurosis in civil life* Psychoneurosis is by no means exclusively a military problem. It occurs with great frequency in civil life and furnishes physicians a large proportion of their incomes even though they frequently fail to make the correct diagnosis....

This is to say that all men are not endowed with an equal amount of courage. Every man has his breaking point and, if pushed beyond it, will develop a psychoneurosis.

c. *Contributory causes* Physical condition exerts a great influence both upon the production and the cure of psychoneurosis. This is often seen in prolonged illnesses, where the courage of the patient and his ability to suffer pain diminish with time. Physical exhaustion markedly decreases a man's courage.

3. *Psychoneurosis in soldiers*

   a. *In other than combat zones* a considerable number of recruits develop a psychoneurosis shortly after induction. These are, in general, people who either have been badly adjusted in civil life, or who were relatively well adjusted to an easy and secure environment. When such were hurriedly removed from surroundings in which they were reasonably secure and placed in a new world full of strange things, their courage was inadequate.

      Movement overseas cracked others who had adjusted fairly well to military service in the Z/I and this cracking continued after arrival overseas, precipitated by such situations as overwork, criticism—friendly or otherwise—by their associates, failure to obtain promotion which the officer or soldier thought his due, nostalgia, and many other irritants real or imagined.

   b. *In combat,* environment is the least healthy of all. Men are killed in plain view of other men. Others are maimed. Greater courage is required to withstand such untoward incidents. Furthermore, physical exhaustion, from long marches and little sleep, is a common state among combat troops.

4. *Prevention of psychoneurosis in soldiers*

   a. *Factors in behavior of soldiers* Perhaps the two most important governing factors in a soldier's behavior are confidence in his leadership and fear. Of these, it is probable that fear is the greater.

   b. *Confidence in leadership* There are only a few people in the world who feel adequate in themselves to face serious crises. Most people, faced with a crisis, turn instinctively to another person in whom they have confidence. There are many soldiers who, left to their own devices, would turn and run from the enemy, but who are held to their duty by a calm and impressive noncommissioned officer. The noncommissioned officer, in turn, must receive moral support from his platoon leader, and he from his company commander. Lack of confidence in his leadership is fatal to the soldier of low courage.

   c. *Fear* It is my opinion that fear is the ultimate dominating factor in human behavior and that, in war, it should be exploited to the fullest extent.

      The noblest application of fear is the fear of being afraid. Undoubtedly every soldier is afraid at some time or another—and many of them are afraid most of the time. But the solider who is more afraid of being afraid—of exhibiting signs of cowardice—than he is afraid of the enemy is a fine type of soldier. This application of fear should be exploited by all commanders.

Unfortunately, however, there is a certain proportion of soldiers who are more afraid of the enemy, and what the enemy can do to them, than they are of being cowardly. Nevertheless, a still more potent fear can be generated in such soldiers; and this the fear of certain punishment which is as bad as the worst the enemy can inflict. If every soldier *knew* that he would be executed for cowardice, for malingering, or for a self-inflicted wound, the vast majority of the weakling would choose the more favorable odds offered in facing the enemy.

So long as the soldier is permitted to malinger, to shoot himself and be cleared of intent in 90 percent of cases, and even permitted to develop a psychoneurosis, we are going to be confronted with this problem. The plain fact is that—aided, abetted and confused by too much psychiatric theory—our War Department and our commanders have not faced this problem in a realistic manner.

I realize how unpopular my opinions are with psychiatrists. Perhaps my opinions are influenced by the fact that I have been a soldier for nearly thirty years. But there is one fact that no psychiatrist can explain—*psychoneurosis is not a problem in the Russian Army.* The Russians punish cowardice with death.

5. *Cure of psychoneurosis*

   a. Since physical exhaustion plays such an important role in the production of psychoneurosis, there is a considerable proportion of cases—not as large as many psychiatrists believe—that are cured with rest, sedatives and good food. These are cases developing in soldiers of some courage, who break not primarily from the emotional strain of combat but for other reasons, such as fatigue, family trouble, or other contributing factors. Such soldiers can be returned to full combat duty; but the great majority of them, under our present system of management, will break again *under similar circumstances.*

   b. There is a small, a very small, group of soldiers who break after months of combat service—not from any one incident or situation but from the cumulative effect of hundreds of days and nights of uncertainty, of exhaustion, and of the presence of death. Many of these soldiers have been outstanding, some decorated for valor.

      These cases are *real.* They have a real psychoneurosis, not a want of courage because they have demonstrated their courage for many months. It is that they have just made too many trips to the well of their courage, and it has temporarily gone dry.

      Some of these cases can be restored to combat duty, but not all—perhaps less than half. But practically all of them can be restored to useful duty, where their great combat experience can be utilized—in training or in the administration of the replacement system in the CZ.

   c. There is next a group of cases of which, under our present system of management, few can ever be restored to combat duty. These soldiers simply do not have sufficient courage—and again I stress the difference between courage and bravery—to support them in combat. They can be restored to some useful service in rear of the immediate fighting—even to labor in the combat zone not far behind the lines.

      The question was asked me by G-1, War Department: "If such men can be restored to labor duty in the combat zone, why cannot they be returned to actual combat duty?"

The answer to this question seems to me to be that it takes more to make a combat soldier than his mere presence in a combat unit; that the very nature of combat requires considerable dispersion of soldiers and some amount of courage, initiative and self-reliance on the part of each combat soldier; whereas laborers can be and are worked in groups—under guard, if necessary—and are not employed in the actual front line.

These men can be made again into combat soldiers only if the fear of summary execution can be made to dominate their fear of injury by the enemy. But, so long as soldiers in this group know that they can continue to escape combat service by developing symptoms, they can never be remade into combat soldiers.

d.   There is a fourth group of psychoneurotics with such profound symptoms as to be actually psychotic. These cases are hopeless from a military standpoint, and should be discharged from the service under SECTION VIII, AR 615–630 at once. This is a relatively small group.

6.   Utilization of psychoneurotics

a.   The group of the milder cases—whom the term "combat exhaustion" fits more nearly than it does the majority of cases—can be and are being returned to combat duty. As a *general* rule, these are the poorer type of soldier, but are usable in combat units.

b.   The second group—those who crack after months of combat—can be and are being rehabilitated for useful service in some capacity.

c.   As regards the third group—those that can under our present system of management be remade into combat soldiers only with great difficulty but who can be salvaged for some useful labor—these constitute the great administrative as well as the great medical problem.

I am unalterably opposed to returning such soldiers to duty in normal units, either combat or service. It must be remembered that there are *potential* psychoneurotics in every unit in the Army and that most of these are deterred from showing symptoms by the example of the better of their comrades. To dilute such units with these weaklings is only to invite an epidemic of psychoneurosis among the soldiers of the unit who, until subjected to this influence, were doing acceptable duty. Such a solution is merely placing rotten apples in barrels of sound ones.

However, organized into special units under specially selected officers and noncommissioned officers and properly administered, some useful work can be had from them and some can be salvaged for full duty.

Such units should be worked hard. They should be quartered and fed under no better conditions than combat troops. There should be no attractive considerations to invite soldiers into such units.

Shame at being a member of such a unit will salvage a certain proportion. Others, without shame, will be content in such a unit for the duration of the war. And perhaps some will deteriorate into the fourth class and have to be discharged.

The point is, however, that the existence of such a problem must be squarely faced sooner or later. It is a command problem. The Medical Department can say—with greater or lesser accuracy—that here is a soldier that is remade into a complete soldier; or that here is a soldier that, under existing restrictions, cannot be remade at this time into a complete soldier but can be used under certain conditions, or that here is a soldier who will always be worthless. The Medical Department also can advise—with complete accuracy—that, if soldiers of the second group are mixed with good soldiers, the standard of the good soldiers will drop appreciably.

Further than this the Medical Department cannot go—nor should it intrude. The problems that face the commander are these:

(1)   Shall I use this middle group that can perform some useful service but cannot all be remade into complete soldiers?

(2)   If I shall use them, should I charge them against my troop basis knowing that they will not be more than 60 percent as effective as good soldiers?

(3)   If I shall not use them, shall they be discharged from the service and replaced with new drafts upon the population?

While the answers to these questions are not the concern of the Medical Department, it seems evident that no commander will voluntarily elect to use such poor material if he is charged with it on his troop basis at the same rate as good material. It would appear, then, that the time has come for the War Department to face this problem realistically by relaxing the rigid limits of troop bases sufficiently to provide some cushion for this poor material.

Paul R. Hawley,
Major General, USA,
Chief Surgeon. (1031–34)

Contemporary Approaches to Trauma

The following excerpt provides guidance for psychiatrists and psychologists in diagnosing their patients. By definition, a person suffering from post-traumatic stress disorder must continue to experience stress related to the trauma long after the traumatic event is over. The person must have believed he or she was in significant danger during the event, but the resulting fear remains even after the danger has passed. This fear can emerge in nightmares or hallucinations, such as when Tayo continues to hear Japanese voices mingled with Laguna ones. The dangerous event impedes the patient's ability to function normally after the danger is over. In part, this may be because a person, once exposed to random or profound violence for example, can lose faith in an orderly universe. Post-traumatic stress disorder is a broader diagnosis than battle fatigue because although soldiers during war are undeniably exposed to trauma, they are not the only ones. A person could also suffer from this disorder as a result of domestic violence, child abuse, violent crime, severe accidents, and so forth.

FROM *DIAGNOSTIC AND STATISTICAL MANUAL OF MENTAL DISORDERS,* "DIAGNOSTIC CRITERIA FOR . . . POSTTRAUMATIC STRESS DISORDER"

(American Psychological Association, 2000)

A. The person has been exposed to a traumatic event in which both of the following were present:

   (1)   the person experienced, witnessed, or was confronted with an event or events that involved actual or threatened death or serious injury, or a threat to the physical integrity of self or others

   (2)   the person's response involved intense fear, helplessness, or horror . . .

B. The traumatic event is persistently reexperienced in one (or more) of the following ways:

   (1)   recurrent and intrusive distressing recollections of the event . . .

   (2)   recurrent distressing dreams of the event . . .

   (3)   acting or feeling as if the traumatic event were recurring (. . . a sense of reliving the experience, illusions, hallucinations, and dissociative flashback episodes, including those that occur on awakening or when intoxicated) . . .

   (4)   intense psychological distress at exposure to . . . cues that . . . resemble . . . the traumatic event

   (5)   physiological reactivity on exposure to . . . cues that . . . resemble . . . the traumatic event

C. Persistent avoidance of stimuli associated with the trauma and numbing of general responsiveness . . . as indicated by three (or more) of the following:

   (1)   efforts to avoid thoughts, feelings, or conversations associated with the trauma

   (2)   efforts to avoid activities, places, or people that arouse recollections of the trauma

   (3)   inability to recall an important aspect of the trauma

   (4)   markedly diminished interest or participation in significant activities

   (5)   feelings of detachment or estrangement . . .

   (6)   restricted range of affect . . .

   (7)   sense of foreshortened future . . .

D. Persistent symptoms of increased arousal . . . as indicated by two (or more) of the following:

(1) difficulty falling or staying asleep

(2) irritability or outbursts of anger

(3) difficulty concentrating

(4) hypervigilance

(5) exaggerated startle response

E. Duration of the disturbance...is more than 1 month.

F. The disturbance causes clinically significant distress or impairment in social, occupational, or other important areas of functioning. (427–29)

ADDITIONAL EXAMPLES OF HEALING CEREMONIES

The next three excerpts provide descriptions of nonfictional accounts of Native American healing ceremonies. These ceremonies share some details with the ceremony Tayo participates in, but each one is distinctly individualized. The ceremonies respond to their contexts; when the context shifts, the details of the ceremony shift also. Elsie Clews Parsons was an anthropologist who did much of her work among the Pueblos near the beginning of the twentieth century. In this text, her emphasis is on what happens; she provides only a little information about why the ceremony is performed this way. The next excerpt is taken from a memoir that attempts to explain the traditions of an entire people—rather than an individual life—and that describes attitudes pertaining to ritual as part of that explanation. The third excerpt involves a contemporary woman who had been adopted out of her tribe; she is unfamiliar with many traditional practices but believes that separation from her relatives has contributed to her condition.

Elsie Clews Parsons' Description of a Ceremony at Laguna Pueblo

In the following excerpt, anthropologist Elsie Clews Parsons describes a ritual performed by a *cheani,* or shaman, to cure a patient whose heart has been stolen by a witch. Illnesses are frequently attributed to such thievery by witches. Notice, however, that Parsons does not claim to have observed this ceremony directly; rather she has been told about it, and she repeats what she has been told. Because many ceremonies are conducted privately, respecting the sacredness of the event, anthropologists sometimes gather information through interview rather than direct observation. Cautious readers will question whether this version is both accurate and complete.

The shaman is attired according to particular traditions, with his clothing, his hairstyle, and his face painting dictated by the parameters of the ceremony. Much of the ritual occurs through symbolic gesture—the waving of the bear claw, the blowing of the pollen toward the patient. In a sense, the shaman acts also as a prophet, allowing the pollen to predict whether the patient will live or die. Since four is a sacred number in Laguna tradition and in other Native American traditions, fewer than four grains of pollen would indicate that the patient is out of harmony with creation. If harmony cannot be restored, the patient will surely die. Many ceremonies, including Tayo's, attempt to maintain or restore harmony among humans, animals, and the rest of creation.

FROM ELSIE CLEWS PARSONS, *NOTES ON
CEREMONIALISM AT LAGUNA*

(Anthropological Papers of the American Museum of Natural History,
Vol. xix, Part iv, 1920)

From the sister of the *shikani cheani* I learned about his curing ceremony—all the
cheani worked cures, being invited with a package of meal. The *cheani* gives the meal
to his *iyatik,* asking her help. He visits the patient for four days before the ceremony.
Kuati, "going after" i.e., of the heart of the patient, the ceremony is called. The heart
is believed to have been carried off by *kanadyeya* (witch, evil spirit), the witch taking
animal form. In the house of the patient the altar is set up facing, preferably, towards
oshà ch gama.

Shikani cheani is nude but for a breechcloth. He has across his nose two lines of red
paint (*hakacha*) and two lines across his lips. There are four lines on each side of his
face. He is painted, like *mà sewi,* or like the representations of *mà sewi,* the "war captains," "because it is through *mà sewi* he hopes for success." His hair is tied in a top
knot and over "the soft place in the head" is painted in red a small cross "to keep away
the evil spirits." An assistant *cheani* ... holds a crystal (*mashanyu,* great light) to the
light, and *shikani cheani* goes about the room as in a daze searching as it were for the
stolen heart. The assistant sings. *Shikani cheani* proceeds to suck places on the body
of the patient. Then having rubbed ashes on his body as a prophylactic against witches
and on the calves of his legs so as not to get tired, with his bear paw in his left hand,
a flint knife in his right, he rushes outdoors, slashing the air with the flint. Two "war
captains" with bow and arrows and a blood relative of the *cheani* with a gun follow
the *cheani* as he goes forth, running so fast that it is with difficulty his companions
keep up with him. He may go to the river for the heart (it is usually found in the river
bank) or he may dig somewhere with his bear claw. In a notable case, he dug up the
girl patient's heart under a cedar. While he is out and, before that, while he is suck-
ing, his assistant sings...

    Returning to the house of the patient, *shikani cheani* creeps in on hands and knees,
clasping in the bear's paw the "heart." The "war captains" take the "heart" from him,
and so violent is his behavior, that the "war captains" have to hold him down. He stiff-
ens into a kind of spasm, and his female relatives have to massage him back to consciousness. They rub him with ashes. Restored, he is given warm water to drink, and
he goes out and vomits. Returning, he takes from the altar the *hishami* of four eagle
feathers and with them rolls up to the patient the "heart," three or four grains of corn
wrapped one by one in red cloth, bound with cotton. He undoes the tangle, searching out the thickly wrapped grains. If there are three grains only, the patient will die,
if four, the patient will recover. In the latter case the *cheani* says, *wachutsa,* "there are
enough." He places the four grains on the palm of his right hand and blows as if blowing them back into the body of the patient. He blows towards the left arm of the patient, then towards the right arm, then towards the left knee and the right knee. After
this, in a shell, he gives the patient the four grains of corn to swallow together with

medicine (*wawa*) from the medicine bowl from the altar. In conclusion, the relatives of the *cheani* wash the heads of the relatives of the patient. (118–22)

Albert Yava's Description of Tradition

In this excerpt, Albert Yava summarizes traditional Pueblo understandings of the world. Life is good, and the sources of life should be honored. Boundaries between types of life, human and animal for instance, are to some extent artificial—although he doesn't claim that humans and animals are the same, he does describe them as relatives of each other. He also expresses concern that such traditional understanding has eroded; even if younger Hopis can perform the dances and care for religious goods properly, they seem to have lost the feeling for these activities. For Yava, the dances and other rituals express an underlying attitude; when that attitude is lost, the meaning of the dance will be lost, too. The dances will become devoid of significance and eventually themselves also lost. Once this occurs, all of life could be subject to destruction. Tayo's experience with the older men in the kiva near the end of the novel represents the passing on of their knowledge to someone who is worthy to receive it. Several of the details Yava mentions are pertinent to *Ceremony*—recognizing the significance of the sun at dawn, shape-shifting from human to bear or deer.

FROM ALBERT YAVA, *BIG FALLING SNOW: A TEWA-HOPI INDIAN'S LIFE AND TIMES AND THE HISTORY AND TRADITIONS OF HIS PEOPLE,* ED. HAROLD COURLANDER

(Crown, 1978)

[W]e old-timers can see that there has been a steady drift away from our traditional attitude toward nature and the universe. What I'm talking about is not the dancing and the kiva paraphernalia, all those visible things. They are only a means of expressing what we feel about the world. I am talking about the feelings and attitudes behind the kiva rituals. We feel that the world is good. We are grateful to be alive. We are conscious that all men are brothers. We sense that we are related to other living creatures. Life is to be valued and preserved. If you see a grain of corn on the ground, pick it up and take care of it, because it has life inside. When you go out of your house in the morning and see the sun rising, pause a moment to think about it. That sun brings warmth to the things that grow in the fields. If there's a cloud in the sky, look at it and remember that it brings rain to a dry land. When you take water from a spring, be aware that it is a gift of nature.

All those stories we tell about men changing into bears or deer, and then changing back...express our certainty that the dividing line between humans and animals is very slim, and that we are here to share what is given to us. We seek a way of communicating with the source of life, so we have prayers and kachinas. I think we are probably as successful at this effort to communicate as Christians are. . . . I believe we are constantly aware that it exists, and that without it we would not be here . . . we have not lost our sense of wonder about the universe and existence. (134)

Carl A. Hammerschlag's Observations of a Contemporary Ceremony

In the next excerpt, Dr. Carl A. Hammerschlag describes a ceremony organized to treat a woman named Mary, who had been removed from her tribe years before and who now desires a reconnection. This ceremony resembles the scene in *Ceremony* when Tayo begins working with Old Betonie. Here, Mary sits in the midst of a sand painting designed to recall someone who "had returned in another form." The prayers are elaborate and set to music, which helps both Mary and the medicine man, as well as observers, remember the words. The ritual places Mary in the midst of heroic figures, intending that she merge with this heroic community. Later, she will remember the blessing that was chanted over her, and this memory will serve to keep the blessing alive.

FROM CARL A. HAMMERSCHLAG, M.D., *THE DANCING HEALERS: A DOCTOR'S JOURNEY OF HEALING WITH NATIVE AMERICANS*

(HarperCollins, 1989)

The ceremony was held in a hogan. Mary was frightened that she would make mistakes and not be able to repeat exactly the words of the prayers. Her sister helped her learn her part in the ritual.

The medicine man knew every word for the entire ceremony in exactly the right order, each line with its appropriate melody. As he sang, he sprinkled multicolored sands on the ground with movements of his thumb and forefinger, creating what many believe to be the greatest folk art on this continent.

Mary stared at the sand painting in awe. It depicted a Navajo legend about a child who was lost to the tribe, but who returned in another form. The medicine man asked Mary to sit in the middle of the painting. Now she could actually mingle with the heroic figures and absorb their strength.

The medicine man tied feathers and spruce on Mary and placed stone and wooden fetishes, holy objects, on her. He twirled a wooden noisemaker and made a huge roar. Mary felt the breeze from this instrument as if it were blowing her old confused and angry self away.

The medicine man gave her a pipe filled with sweet tobacco. He smoked it; she smoked it; and they blew clouds of tobacco smoke over themselves and toward the sky. For everyone, the atmosphere was charged with feeling.

Mary kept the parts of herself in alignment by remembering the words sung in her ceremony:

> Happily—may you walk with God—
>
> Happily—may you walk—
>
> Happily—may you feel light within—
>
> Happily—with feeling may you walk—
>
> Happily—may you walk with God. (46–47)

TENSIONS AND CONNECTIONS AMONG TRADITIONS

The next two documents describe the ways in which physicians and traditional healers are both different and similar. Lori Arviso Alvord, a Navajo surgeon, was forced to defy some of her ingrained beliefs as part of her medical training. She literally embodies both the strengths of each system and also the numerous ways they reject each other. Such tensions often occur when extremely different cultures encounter each other, especially when individual members of one culture attempt to adapt to the other. In the second passage, Richard Selzer, also a surgeon, compares his work to that of a shaman. Although most of his points of comparison depend on metaphor, his goal is to demonstrate that the two traditions aren't as diametrically opposed as many might think.

Lori Arviso Alvord's Experiences in Medical School

The following document is an excerpt from a memoir describing how Lori Alvord was able to negotiate medical school while also retaining some of her traditional beliefs. Because different cultures subscribe to different taboos, adapting to one culture can mean violating the taboos of another. In Alvord's case, she had to dissect human corpses if she expected to succeed in medical school, but Navajo tradition had taught her that evil would be released into her life if she did so. She is able to dissect her cadaver by responding to two somewhat different ideas: first, the cadaver, after being preserved in formaldehyde, looks very different from a living human being, and second, her desire to heal people outweighed her fear of the taboo. Nevertheless, before she can make her first incision, she must consciously insist on denying her fear. This passage illustrates not simply the differing belief systems of the two cultures but also provides a vivid example of how a belief system influences areas of life beyond religion—education, for instance.

FROM LORI ARVISO ALVORD, M.D., AND ELIZABETH COHEN VAN PELT, *THE SCALPEL AND THE SILVER BEAR: THE FIRST NAVAJO WOMAN SURGEON COMBINES WESTERN MEDICINE AND TRADITIONAL HEALING*

(Bantam Books, 2000)

Navajos do not touch the dead. Ever.

It is one of the strongest rules of our culture. The dead hold *ch'įįdis,* or evil spirits, that are simply not to be tampered with. When a person dies, the "good" part of the person leaves with the spirit, while the "evil" part stays with the physical body....

In medical school this taboo confronted me on every level. Never before had I been asked to do anything that directly violated the beliefs of my culture.... If I wanted to become a doctor, I had to dissect.

Standing in front of my cadaver I thought back on stories about this person and that person who had touched a dead thing, and the consequences that befell them.

I thought about all the *ch'įįndis* of all the dead people around me in that lab room....

There below me was an older male of medium build. His skin was shriveled and toughened by formaldehyde, a slate-gray color that I'd never seen on a living person.... Its "non-human" appearance helped me forget that this had once been a real, breathing home for a human soul....

Okay, I thought. *This is what I want, the knowledge I will acquire here is like that of a medicine man. I will be able to bring home a tremendous gift. And if I am good enough, my work could even fight processes that cause death. In the course of a career, I could help thousands of my people.*

Cast in this light, my decision became easier. I took a deep breath. Someone handed me a scalpel. *I'm not afraid,* I told myself. *I'm not afraid.* I reached down to the shape below me and slid the scalpel into the skin. (40–43)

Richard Selzer's Comparison of Shamans and Surgeons

In the following document, taken from an essay by surgeon Richard Selzer, the author begins by describing an extreme difference in the training of shamans and surgeons—a person had to die and be cannibalized before being resurrected as a shaman. Such an experience seems initially unlike anything a surgeon experiences. Yet surgeons also participate in rites of passage and other rituals. A primary difference, Selzer implies, is that surgeons, prior to any operation, try to eliminate all areas of the unknown. Surgery will most likely be successful if the surgeon doesn't encounter any surprises. Selzer states that a surgeon's knowledge sometimes contributes to an unfortunate arrogance, and suggests that a more reverent attitude, reminiscent of a shaman's, can only occur if a surgeon is willing to acknowledge the unknown details of the life before him. Ironically, surgeons will only become like gods if they forsake the arrogance that sometimes indicates they expect to be treated as gods.

FROM RICHARD SELZER, *TAKING THE WORLD IN FOR REPAIRS*

(Penguin, 1987)

Time was when, in order to become a shaman, one had to undergo an initiatory death and resurrection. The aspirant had to be taken to the sky or the netherworld; often he would be dismembered by spirits, cooked in a pot and eaten by them. Only then could he be born again as a shaman. No such rite of passage goes into the making of a surgeon . . . but there is something about the process of surgical training that is reminiscent of the sacred ur-drama after all. After a number of years of abasement and humiliation he or she is led to a room where no one else is permitted. There is the donning of special raiment, the washing of the hands and, at last, the performance of secret rites before the open ark of the body . . .

The shaman's journey through disorder and illness to health has parallels to the surgeon's journey into the body. . . . What is different is that the surgeon practices inherited rites, while the shaman is susceptible to visions. Still, they both perform acts bent upon making chaos into cosmos.

Ritual has receded from the act of surgery. Only the flavor of it is left, giving, if not to the performers, then to the patients and to those forbidden to witness these events, a shiver of mysticism. Few and far between are the surgeons who consider what they do an encounter with the unknown. When all is said and done, I am left with the suspicion that we have gone too far in our arrogant drift from the priestly forebears of surgery. It is pleasing to imagine surgeons bending over their incisions with love, infusing them with the impalpable. Only then would the surgeon, like the shaman, turn himself into a small god and re-create the world. (213–14)

A RESPONSE TO PRAYER AS MEDICINE

The final document is an editorial that raises questions about the relationship between prayer and science. The writer isn't questioning whether prayer can help cure illness; rather, the editorial suggests that believing prayer is effective only if science says so contradicts the essence of faith. Truly faithful people should not need to rely on objective measures to quantify the value of faith, nor should they perceive their faith as valuable only if its results can be empirically measured. Simultaneously, when one desires prayer to be validated by science, one grants the discourse and values of science more authority than the values of faith. In addition, some studies attribute the apparent health benefits of faith to details often correlated with church attendance—a satisfactory social life, for instance. The writer also notes the condescending tone with which science often addresses faith, as if people of faith aren't quite smart enough to participate in scientific exchange—and objections to tone lead the writer to insights about objections to content. The editorial also ironically suggests that nonbelievers will start attending church for the same reason they take their daily vitamins, rather than for the reasons churches themselves actually try to appeal to their members—but such a response to these studies is, of course, unlikely. Although Tayo has accepted treatment through Western medicine before he turns to religious ritual, he approaches his ceremony reverently if not, in the beginning, hopefully. His willingness to accept the conditions and inconveniences of the ceremony contribute to its value; he is not treating it as a commodity, as the authors of this editorial also suggest believers should not treat prayer as a commodity.

"FAITH'S BENEFITS"

(*Christian Century*, Jan. 27, 1999, 116:3)

It seems that every few weeks we read another report touting the health benefits of being religious. Scientists have discovered, for example, that people who study the Bible, pray and go to church are less likely to have high blood pressure. Another study has found that smokers who go to church live longer than smokers who don't. One researcher has summed it up: "If you're a smoker, get your butt in church."

Linda George, a sociology professor at Duke, observes that "religious people have better support systems, which keep them healthier," and she suggests that "the sense of meaning and kind of comfort that religious beliefs provide make them more resistant to stresses, both physical and social." The interaction of faith and medicine is increasingly recognized as a legitimate area of scientific research. Dale Matthews of Georgetown Medical School notes that "the faith factor has been demonstrated to have value."

The media's accounts of these findings invariably take a solicitous tone toward the faithful, as if believers are bound to be gratified by medical evidence of religion's utilitarian value. In pondering why we were irritated by that tone, we realized why we are ambivalent about these reports. It's not that we don't think spiritual and physical health are somehow aligned (they certainly went together in Jesus' ministry); and it's not that we don't think the interaction of body and soul is a subject worthy of investigation. It's just that we don't like to see the therapists of well-being ushering people to the pews.

Perhaps no one is so simple as to start treating church like a nutritional supplement or a leafy green vegetable—something to add to one's life just to be on the safe side. Nevertheless, with their medically authorized praise of religion, the scientists subtly confirm their own cultural authority. In our society, it's the scientists, not the tellers of sacred stories, that get to define the "value" of the "faith factor." Their reports further inject the dangerous notion that faith is validated by its measurable outcomes. As long as one takes this view of faith, one will never get started on the actual journey of faith.

So we can be only halfheartedly enthusiastic about the prospect of scientists conducting tests to demonstrate the power of prayer or the clinical uses of forgiveness. As Kierkegaard once said, when we try to suck worldly wisdom from the movements of faith, we tend to swindle God out of the first movement.

TOPICS FOR WRITTEN OR ORAL EXPLORATION

1. Compare the mythology present in *Ceremony* with that present in other novels or memoirs that respond directly to a culture's mythic system. Examples include *The Woman Warrior* by Maxine Hong Kingston, *Parable of the Sower* by Octavia Butler, and *Song of Solomon* by Toni Morrison.

2. Write an essay in which you trace the various factors that contribute to Tayo's psychological condition. How are his experiences during the war related to his experiences previous to joining the military?

3. Write an essay in which you compare Tayo's response to the war with Harley's or Emo's.

4. Research the mythology of another culture. What other stories can you find that describe how medicine was introduced to a culture?

5. Write a response to Major General Hawley, either agreeing or disagreeing with his interpretations and stating why.

6. Compare Major General Hawley's suggestions in his memorandum to the suggestions Jonathan Swift makes in his essay "A Modest Proposal." What do the suggestions have in common? How do we know that the intentions of the two writers are not similar? How might Jonathan Swift respond to the problem of battle fatigue?

7. Use the criteria from the *Diagnostic and Statistical Manual of Mental Disorders* to analyze Tayo's condition. According to the criteria listed, does Tayo suffer from post-traumatic stress disorder?

8. Interview a psychologist or psychiatrist about their experiences with people suffering from post-traumatic stress disorder. What treatments does he or she recommend, and why? Alternately, interview an alternative healer, asking similar questions about his or her practice.

9. Research a particular type of alternative medicine, such as acupuncture, homeopathy, herbal supplements, sweat lodges, and so forth.

10. Examine the catalogs of several American medical schools. Which ones offer future doctors training in alternative medical practices? Which alternative practices do they emphasize?

11. Do a survey of people in your town or neighborhood regarding their use of alternative or complementary medicines. To protect their privacy, you may design the survey so that it can be completed anonymously.

12. Interview your family physician about his or her attitudes toward alternative or complementary medicine. What advice would your doctor give you if you were considering such alternative treatment?

13. Write an essay describing the ways in which contemporary Western medicine also contains ritual. You might begin by thinking about the aspects of a doctor's appointment or hospital stay that occur in basically the same way every time.

14. Compare the ceremony Tayo completes with the descriptions of the other cere-

monies included here. What details do the various ceremonies share? Why? In what ways do they differ? What factors might influence those differences?

15. Organize a debate in your class on the appropriate role of religion and medicine in controversial social issues. For example, should a priest or a doctor decide whether a woman should have an abortion? whether extraordinary measures such as feeding tubes or respirators should prolong the life of a person who would otherwise die? What is the appropriate role of politicians in these controversies?

16. Write an essay examining your own religious experience(s). Which elements of religion are ceremonial? How significant is ritual to religion?

SUGGESTED READING

Anderson, Robert S., ed. *Neuropsychiatry in World War II.* Washington: U.S. Government Printing Office, 1966.

Archives of Internal Medicine, 26 June 2000: Special issue on prayer and medicine. 160.12.

Cooke, Elliott Duncan. *All but Me and Thee: Psychiatry at the Foxhole Level.* Washington: Infantry Journal Press, 1946.

Dossey, L. *Healing Words: The Power of Prayer and the Practice of Medicine.* New York: HarperCollins, 1993.

Giger, Joyce Newman, and Ruth Elaine Davidhizar. *Transcultural Nursing: Assessment and Intervention.* 3rd ed. St. Louis: Mosby, 1999.

Manninger, William C. *Psychiatry in a Troubled World: Yesterday's War and Today's Challenge.* New York: MacMillan, 1948.

Mehl-Madrona, Lewis. *Coyote Medicine: Lessons from Native American Healing.* New York: Simon & Schuster, 1998.

Meisenhelder, Janice Bell, and Emily N. Chandler. "Faith, Prayer and Health Outcomes in Elderly Native Americans." *Clinical Nursing Research* 9 (2000): 191–204.

Mohatt, Gerald Vincent, and Joseph Eagle Elk. *The Price of a Gift: A Lakota Healer's Story.* Lincoln: Bison Books, 2002.

Neihardt, John G. *Black Elk Speaks: Being the Life Story of a Holy Man of the Ogalala Sioux.* New York: MJF Books, 1961.

Purnell, Larry D., and Betty J. Paulanka. *Transcultural Health Care: A Culturally Competent Approach.* Philadelphia: F.A. Davis Co., 1998.

Radin, Paul. *The Autobiography of a Winnebago Indian: Life, Ways, Acculturation, and the Peyote Cult.* New York: Dover, 1963.

Shephard, Ben. *A War of Nerves: Soldiers and Psychiatrists in the Twentieth Century.* Cambridge: Harvard University Press, 2001.

Simmons, Leo W., ed. *Sun Chief: The Autobiography of a Hopi Indian.* New Haven: Yale University Press, 1942.

Sloan, R., E. Bagiella, and T. Powell. "Religion, Spirituality, and Medicine." *The Lancet* 353 (1999): 664.

Vogel, Virgil J. *American Indian Medicine.* Norman: University of Oklahoma Press, 1970.

5

Native Americans, Alcohol, and Social Welfare

CEREMONY AND ALCOHOL

Among the most consistent habits of several characters in *Ceremony,* especially those of Tayo's generation, is alcohol use and abuse. Harley willingly tolerates great inconvenience to satisfy his desire for beer; in his drunken exploits, he is frequently accompanied by Emo. Both Harley and Emo, in fact, generally populate scenes in which alcohol inhabits the center of the social circle. Although Tayo isn't as compelled by alcohol—he isn't an alcoholic and he doesn't initiate drinking binges—he nevertheless accepts his friends' behavior as normal, or at least inevitable, for much of the novel. And he—sometimes passively, sometimes actively—accepts his own attachment to that milieu. Throughout *Ceremony,* alcohol use is linked to the characters' harsh circumstances and plays a role in several unfortunate incidents.

Tayo's exposure to the consequences of alcohol abuse has begun long before the novel opens. All Tayo absolutely knows about his father is that he was white. Based on his mother's behavior, however, Tayo and his maternal relatives surmise a few other details about his father's identity; he was likely similar to the drunk white men who stumble into the arroyo in Gallup looking for quick, cheap sex. The one story Tayo's aunt tells him about his mother involves her stumbling home naked save for her shoes; although no one ever reveals exactly what events preceded this moment, alcohol was surely a factor. Tayo's mother's addiction both causes her to do things she would not otherwise do and permits her to engage in her own humiliation. She surely did not set out to become an alcoholic or a mother who would neglect and abandon her son. Absent as she is from much of the text, she is mirrored in the character of Helen Jean, who left the reservation searching for a more exciting life, and who discovered that such a life was not open to her. Through the section of the novel set in the arroyo, readers understand that Tayo's mother is far from unique—that desperation (whether because of addictions or other reasons) reduces many people to primitive behavior.

For Tayo's mother and, by extension, for several of the Native American characters, addiction begins in the shame of identity. His mother doesn't simply become ashamed of the actions she commits while drunk, but rather, she becomes drunk because of her shame at who she is—a Native American. Although as a young woman she acquires white habits of fashion and conduct, she soon realizes that while she may be able to imitate white people, those same white people will always classify her as Native American. Following that realization, "She hated the people at home when white people talked about their peculiarities; but she always hated herself more because she still thought about them, because she knew their pain at what she was doing with her life. The feelings of shame, at her own people and at the white people, grew inside her, side by side like monstrous twins that would have to be left in the hills to die" (69). She uses alcohol as a means of masking her shame, until eventually her alcohol use also becomes an additional source of shame. Her addiction, in other words, is only one aspect of the vicious cycle that is her life.

For other characters, alcohol use fulfills similar, though not identical, needs. When Harley, Emo, Tayo, and other veterans socialize, alcohol provides one element in their obsessive ritual. They drink and tell war stories, stories that inevitably involve white women who found them desirable as long as they wore uniforms. Alcohol transports these men back to a moment when they felt like acceptable and genuine Americans, a feeling that evaporated as soon as the war ended and they returned to their reservation and civilian—that is, Native American—identities. They drink both to remember who they were and to forget who they are. Unfortunately, alcohol also prompts these characters to commit acts they would be much less likely to perpetrate sober.

The most startling of these events is Tayo's attempt to kill Emo. The two have been drinking among a group of others, and Emo has provided a gruesome bit of entertainment, placing a handful of teeth from a Japanese corpse into his own mouth. Repulsed, Tayo screams at Emo, who responds with a pair of insults evoking Tayo's mixed ancestry. Both insults rely on stereotypes: the drunken Native American and "white trash." Because of his mixed race, in other words, Tayo endures descriptions of the negative stereotypes of both races but is credited with the stereotypic virtues of neither. Then Emo insults Tayo's mother and accuses Tayo of loving "Japs" (63). Tayo's attitude toward the Japanese is complicated, for Japanese soldiers killed Rocky, but Tayo also recognized his uncle in Japanese prisoners. Rather than attempt to understand his ambivalence or disregard Emo's gratuitous cruelty, Tayo shoves a broken bottle into Emo's belly. Emo survives, and Tayo's crime is attributed to his psychological condition rather than to his drinking. At the climax of the novel, Tayo is again tempted to kill Emo—he even imagines thrusting a screwdriver into Emo's skull—but he resists that temptation. Many factors contribute to Tayo's restraint during this scene, including his improving psychological health, but it is no simple coincidence that he's also sober. In fact, sobriety seems to be a prerequisite to his spiritual recovery.

Not all of the scenes involving alcohol are as disturbing as these that feature so much violence. Yet alcohol is never portrayed as a simple social pleasure, nor do the characters perceive it as a means of enhancing an experience that is already positive in itself. They do not serve a nice wine with dinner or raise a champagne flute to toast a friend's success. Rather, they drink with the sole intent of getting drunk. Drinking, for them, is an end in itself, sometimes the only end worth pursuing. For example, early in the novel, Harley has been banished to the ranch by his family, who hope isolation will keep him out of trouble. He tells Tayo that he plans to ride a burro 30 miles to the boundary of the reservation, to Route 66 and its string of bars. On one level, this scene is comical, and even Harley cracks jokes about his situation. The comedy is superficial, however; Harley's desperation also renders him pitiful, and his attitude reveals that he has surrendered to hopelessness. Throughout *Ceremony*, alcohol use leads inevitably toward physical, spiritual, and cultural dissolution.

CEREMONY AND SOCIAL WELFARE

In addition to problems with alcohol, *Ceremony* also reveals several other demoralizing aspects of Native American life. While these issues aren't foregrounded to the extent alcohol abuse is, the characters' lives are dramatically affected by their social positions and class. Such issues as crime, poverty, and access to education influence the ability of Tayo, his family members, and other residents of Laguna to participate in the "American dream," even if they don't wholeheartedly subscribe to that dream. These problems are strongly correlated with their ethnic identity; that is, they are poor, in part, because they are Native Americans—historical forces and contemporary government policy cooperate to guarantee that most Native Americans will continue to struggle to meet their basic needs. Of course, if the characters had been white, they might also have been poor, but their options would likely have been more numerous. White characters would not likely have been forced to choose between their traditional cultural values and conventional success or status.

The most extended segment of the novel that directly illustrates the poverty in which some of the characters live is the section that occurs in Gallup's arroyo. The narrator describes a shantytown with dwellings made of cast-off materials, including items as flimsy as cardboard. The children who live there are fed by having food "thrown" to them by adults or by scavenging through garbage (108). When the women leave for the evening, presumably to solicit men, the children are left to fend for themselves. All residents of the arroyo make easy targets for white men in search of victims, and for the police.

The residents of the arroyo represent the most extreme edge of poverty, and they are not typical of people who live at Laguna. Even there, however, luxuries are few and generally include what many people would define as necessities. Tayo's grandmother, for example, has been able to use some of the insurance money the family received after Rocky's death to purchase a kerosene stove so she won't have to rely exclusively on the pot-bellied woodstove for heat during the winter. Automobiles are scarce on the reservation, and those that do exist are generally old and unreliable. Even during the late 1940s, most American families would have owned more modern conveniences, although rural areas such as Laguna are seldom as well served as more metropolitan areas. The novel presents the material circumstances at Laguna comparatively objectively—it does not comment on them or render obvious judgment. Material wealth at Laguna itself is not a source of any of the major conflicts, even if the lack of some types of opportunity is what turns a few of the characters toward brighter lights in bigger cities.

The nature of education, however, does elicit judgment and does illustrate a conflict between traditional and Western beliefs, as discussed in the previous chapter. One of the primary functions of the local school is to dissuade Pueblo children of the validity of their traditional beliefs. The teachers are generally white, and to some degree they succeed in persuading their students that scientific beliefs are superior to all others. References are also made to off-reservation schools, such as the Sherman Institute attended by Old Betonie. Although schools like Sherman were intended to force Native American children to abandon traditional culture and adopt white customs of language, dress, and religion, and although Old Betonie attended specifically to learn English, his motive was not to abandon traditional culture but to enhance his ability to perform the ceremonies that keep the world alive. "It," his mother told him when she urged him to go, "It"—that is, evil, witchery—"is carried on in all languages now" (122). Ironically, then, Old Betonie has attended Sherman and learned English, but that experience has extended his capacity in fulfilling his cultural role and responsibility. He was able to acquire the skills he would need without succumbing to the ideology that provided the foundation of schools like Sherman.

Much of the witchery that Old Betonie uses English to counteract is expressed through crime, often violent crime. Even when the witchery is not legally criminal, it is generally violent, as with the war. Yet to a great extent, the characters function outside the criminal justice system. Crimes occur daily in the arroyo for instance, but the police seem to ignore the entire situation, as if it exists outside their jurisdiction, except for the occasional moments when they decide to "clean it up." Then, their goal is simply to save the city embarrassment rather than to assist any victims. When Tayo attempts to kill Emo with the broken bottle, the police intervene, but they decide his precarious psychological state precludes his culpability, which is a valid response but not the only one possible. (One could argue that Tayo's attempted murder of Emo is not only sane but reasonable, given the context.)

When Tayo trespasses on the white rancher's land, however, he is threatened with criminal prosecution. Ironically, this is one of the few crimes in the novel that is simply a crime against property rather than an assault or a murder—for one tension in the novel concerns the value of property over life and the distinctions between mainstream American and traditional Native American understandings of property. Readers understand that the white rancher who owns the land is also guilty of stealing Josiah's property. Objectively, trespassing is a less serious crime than theft of hundreds or even thousands of dollars worth of cattle, but the novel suggests that Tayo is much more likely to be convicted of trespassing than the rancher is of theft. Tayo is threatened with jail, however, not because trespassing is so profoundly serious, but because his accusers operate within an ideological system that assumes involving the police in a criminal matter is the logical, even natural, course of action. Tayo, on the other hand, understands justice differently—he doesn't demand that the rancher be arrested (assuming such a demand would be taken seriously); he simply gets his cattle back.

The novel concludes with a similar expression of justice. Although Emo and Pinkie have tortured Harley to death with Tayo as their witness, they initially seem to escape punishment. In fact, the BIA police have intervened only by attempting to capture Tayo. Yet Emo eventually kills Pinkie, shooting him in the back of the head, and though the FBI defines the event as an accident, citing the alcohol involved, Tayo suspects that Emo has willfully murdered Pinkie. Emo, after all, thrives on violence, and Pinkie's mere existence would remind him of his crimes against Harley. Because Emo is not arrested for the shooting, one could argue that he escapes accountability. He is, however, banished from Laguna; that is, he is ostracized from his home and culture and hence from his own identity. The leaders of Laguna have enforced their own justice, not by wreaking vengeance on Emo, but by exercising their right to define their culture's own boundaries, by insisting that membership in the commu-

nity compels respect for communal values. Those who refuse to adhere to Laguna's values relinquish their place in the community.

NATIVE AMERICANS AND ALCOHOL

Stereotypes regarding Native Americans' use of alcohol began to flourish very
early in American history, before, in fact, the United States existed as an independent country. These stereotypes include the suggestion that Native Americans are particularly prone to alcoholism—an idea that remains debatable in
the medical community—and the simultaneous and paradoxical belief that Native Americans cannot hold their liquor; that they quickly and frequently become falling down drunk. As with all stereotypes, one can easily point to
individuals whose lives support these ideas and to individuals whose lives
strongly contradict them. Regardless of their basis in fact, however, stereotypes
carry significant cultural weight, often becoming internalized even by their objects, as when Harley jokes about drunk Native Americans in *Ceremony*. Nevertheless, alcoholism is a serious problem among Native Americans, to the
extent that some tribes have renewed their active discouragement of alcohol use
by their members, urging instead a return to traditional tribal practices.

Alcohol was introduced to Native Americans through European contact.
Prior to this period, alcohol was relatively unknown to Native Americans (some
tribes, especially those in the West, produced fermented drinks similar to wine,
but none produced distilled liquors such as whiskey), and other intoxicating
substances such as peyote were incorporated into religious rituals only. Because
of their ceremonial value, these substances were not abused as means to quick
inebriation. They were and are treated as sacred, and abuse of them would
have been perceived not simply as substance abuse but also as sacrilegious. Although European Christians used alcohol as part of a religious ritual, many of
them also incorporated it into their ordinary daily lives. Alcohol, in other
words, has never been set aside as an exclusively sacred substance, and Native
Americans were likely introduced to it through its secular rather than religious
function. One theory holds that the Europeans who introduced Native Americans to alcohol were those who were themselves most likely to abuse it, trap-
pers and soldiers and traders who lived on the frontier, apart from peer pressure
to behave well or social judgment when they did not. The Europeans who
taught Native Americans to drink, in other words, taught them to drink expressly in order to get drunk; these Europeans modeled drunkenness as the
expected response to alcohol. While this theory does not likely account for all
alcohol use among Native Americans during the seventeenth through nineteenth centuries, for there were certainly also European models of sobriety, it
is at least partially valid.

Ideas about why some Native Americans originally began to drink so heavily are not in themselves, however, sufficient to address contemporary problems. Alcoholism and other addictions have reached epidemic proportions among Native Americans, although specific rates vary from tribe to tribe and reservation to reservation. Some tribes are less likely than others to accept behavior that does not conform to their traditional values, and particular socioeconomic conditions on reservations are affiliated with differing drinking patterns. Many researchers believe that genetic factors can predispose a person to alcoholism. If this is true, it would be reasonable to suspect that those genetic markers would vary in frequency among ethnic groups; perhaps Native Americans, therefore, are more biologically susceptible to this addiction. Native Americans themselves fervently believe that the systematic destruction of their traditional cultures is a significant factor in the level of addictions in their communities, a suggestion born out by the shame many of the characters in *Ceremony* feel about their identities. Unfortunately, these problems are unlikely to be solved soon, since Native American youth have adopted the habits of their parents and grandparents. Studies of alcohol and drug use among high school students have shown that although approximately the same percentage of Native American students have tried alcohol as their non–Native American peers, Native American teenagers who drink consume greater quantities and do so more often.

Whether or not Native American adults drink more heavily than do adults in the general population (among some tribes, this is almost certainly true), Native Americans unequivocally suffer more damaging consequences from drinking. Cirrhosis and other liver diseases are nearly four times as prevalent in Native Americans as in the general population. Alcohol-related accidents, suicide, and homicide all occur at greater rates in Native American populations than in the population at large. Between 1990 and 1994, 73.2 percent of automobile fatalities among Native Americans were alcohol related. This percentage is substantially higher than that for any other ethnic group—the next highest rate was 59.7 percent among Mexican-Americans, while the average for all Americans was 45.8 percent.

Perhaps one of the most discouraging consequences of excessive alcohol use among Native Americans has been the increasing prevalence of fetal alcohol syndrome (FAS) and its less severe form, fetal alcohol effect (FAE). These conditions occur in children born to mothers who drank when they were pregnant. FAS exhibits itself in a number of physical, psychological, and mental disabilities and conditions. Children with FAS often display facial features that are flattened or sunken and may also have a smaller than normal skull. Their internal organs may also be deformed. They suffer a range of learning disabilities, sometimes beginning with toilet training. In school, they may not understand abstract concepts, so material as basic as multiplication or as significant as government processes may be incomprehensible. As they grow, they often exhibit poor judgment and an inability to associate actions with their consequences; they struggle with concepts like "the future." For example, they may not be able to understand that if they spend their lunch money on candy before school starts, they won't have a lunch at lunchtime. As adults, women with FAS won't understand that if they themselves drink when they are pregnant, serious consequences will become apparent in nine months, and so they may almost unavoidably create a next generation of children with FAS. None of these disabilities can be cured after birth.

FAS is an equal-opportunity condition—it affects children regardless of race or ethnicity. Yet it is currently significantly more prevalent among Native Americans than among the population at large because the drinking patterns of Native American women are different from those of women in other ethnic groups. At this point, scientists have begun to understand how and when exposure to alcohol is most harmful to a fetus—binge drinking is almost certainly always dangerous, but at some stages of development, even one drink by the mother will prove detrimental to the fetus. Babies born to women who have been drinking heavily for years are often more severely affected than babies born to women who are comparatively young in their drinking lives. Because physicians cannot predict exactly how a particular baby will be affected if his or her mother drinks alcohol during pregnancy, the only absolutely safe choice for pregnant women is complete abstinence.

Treatment options for alcohol and other drug abuse range from meetings or support groups, such as Alcoholics Anonymous (AA), which often easily fit into a recovering addict's ordinary schedule, to intensive residential long-term—a year or more—in-patient programs. Most people attempting to recover from addictions will initially try the least-disruptive options, AA or counseling. If the recovery is unsuccessful, an addict might then enroll in a 28-day residential program, which aims to help a person make more thorough lifestyle changes. Some private insurance companies will pay for these 28-day programs. Many addicts eventually require more intense treatment, especially if they have been convicted of serious crimes. A judge may sentence them to a treatment facility in lieu of prison; if they leave treatment early or against clinical advice, they will serve their prison terms.

People who currently work in alcohol and drug recovery programs refer to Native American addicts as being affected by "compound trauma." This term is used to describe people whose addictions are multigenerational and related to traumas their entire cultures—rather than isolated individuals—have suffered. For example, African Americans continue to be affected by the cultural and historical significance of slavery and discrimination. Factors affecting the compound trauma of Native Americans include the decimation of large portions of their population through smallpox and other European diseases, removal to reservations hundreds or thousands of miles from their traditional geographical areas, and separation of families due to forced enrollment of children in boarding schools. When a person's addiction is informed by compound trauma, any successful treatment program would necessarily include a component specifically addressing that trauma. For this reason, some treatment organizations design a specialized track expressly for Native Americans.

NATIVE AMERICANS AND SOCIAL WELFARE

Many statistics indicate that reservations are among the poorest places in the United States. Circumstances can vary dramatically from reservation to reservation, however, depending on such factors as geographic location; whether the reservation encompasses original tribal land, as Pueblo reservations do; whether a tribe operates a casino; and whether a tribe holds mineral rights to oil, uranium, or other resources. Most of the largest reservations are situated on land that proved unattractive to other Americans when the reservation was established, because, for example, it was too dry for substantial agriculture. In addition, rural areas where most reservations are located tend to be poorer than urban areas, although there is, of course, substantial dire poverty in urban areas of the United States also. Unfortunately, poverty is affiliated with a number of other social issues: poor health care, insufficient education, inadequate housing, malnutrition, and so forth. Addressing one aspect of poverty seldom provides a long-term solution if other aspects are not also addressed.

According to the 2000 United States Census, poverty at Laguna was not as dire as on some other reservations. Yet of 231 families, 25.2 percent lived below the poverty level. That figure climbs, however, in families with children and especially families with children when the head of the household was a woman. Of the 30 families with a female head of the household and children younger than five years old, 43.5 percent lived below poverty level. The median household income was $27,664, although 192 (17.7%) households had an annual income of less than $10,000. Only 55 households (5%) had an annual income greater than $75,000.

Houses on Laguna tend to be comparatively small, with an average of five rooms, although 21.2 percent of the houses contain three or fewer rooms. These houses can be crowded, with 11 percent sheltering 1 person to 1.5 persons per room and 5 percent sheltering more than 1.5 persons per room; that is, a three-room house might be the home for six or more people. Many of these houses are valued at less than $50,000, and only 14.9 percent are valued at greater than $100,000. Most striking, perhaps, is the fact that 3.3 percent lack complete plumbing facilities, and 3.4 percent lack complete kitchen facilities, while 11.4 percent lack telephone service. Many of these houses, in other words, might lack hot water or modern toilet facilities. Yet at nearby Acoma, 12.5 percent lack complete plumbing facilities, and on the Hopi reservation, located in Arizona, 46.7 percent of households lack complete plumbing facilities. Nationally, fewer than 1 percent of households lack complete plumbing facilities; even in rural areas that might be more analogous to reservations, fewer than 2 percent of households lack complete plumbing facilities.

Because reservations are often comparatively isolated from large metropolitan areas, adequate health care can be difficult to obtain. Most major hospitals, those that are most technologically advanced, are located in large cities. Reservations are served by the Indian Health Service (IHS), an organization established in 1955. The IHS operates hospitals and clinics and currently cares for approximately 1.6 million Native Americans on a budget that is at best inadequate. Yet because, in part, of poor living conditions (e.g., poor sanitation facilities), Native Americans tend to suffer from greater health problems than other Americans. They contract diseases such as diabetes and tuberculosis at a higher rate than the general population. Among some tribes, diabetes is a particular problem, for if it is untreated or inadequately treated—and often even when it is properly treated—it can lead to blindness and kidney disease, as well as necessitate the amputation of limbs.

Education, also, presents particular challenges among Native American communities. Currently, Native American students drop out of high school at a higher rate than other students. While tribal colleges exist on some reservations, they are generally poorly funded. In addition, the entire history of Native American education is fraught with tension. During the nineteenth century, many well-intended (but by contemporary standards, misguided) individuals believed that the best way to help Native Americans succeed in mainstream culture was to deny them access to their own cultures. Boarding schools were established far from reservations and Native American children required to attend. There, they wore military-style uniforms and had their hair cut; they were forbidden to speak their tribal languages and were seldom permitted to visit their families. As Richard H. Pratt, an influential "friend of the Indian" frequently asserted, one must "kill the Indian, [to] save the man." Pratt and others who shared his view believed that Native Americans would completely die out unless they adapted to white culture. He established the Carlisle Indian School in Pennsylvania in 1879, and it became a model for similar schools. At these boarding schools, Native American children were frequently unhappy, sometimes miserable. They often ran away, although they were nearly always caught and returned to the school. The schools seem to have succeeded only in creating additional ill will toward white authorities. Many differences remain between traditional Native American views of education and more mainstream American ones; these differences include not only what content should be emphasized but also how education should be delivered.

The following documents present a range of views and ideas related to Native Americans and alcohol, as well as about Native Americans and other issues of social welfare. First, four excerpts illustrate stereotypes regarding Native American drinking patterns; these excerpts cover several centuries and conclude at the present. Next, a law passed in 1862 is excerpted that specifically forbids the sale of alcohol to Native Americans on reservations or in "Indian country." Following this, three excerpts illustrate personal experiences of Native Americans with alcohol. Ira Hayes was a hero from World War II who, upon his return to the United States, was unable to control his drinking. As a result, he lost several jobs and was repeatedly arrested. Michael Dorris was an adoptive father who brought the issues of FAS to the public consciousness. Then a table illustrates survey results of Native American teenagers' experience with drugs and alcohol. The last of the excerpts specifically addressing alcohol issues is from a court case involving the Hornell Brewing Company, which marketed a malt liquor called "Crazy Horse" after a revered Sioux chief. Subsequently, two passages discuss the issue of boarding schools for Native Americans during the nineteenth century. The final passage is a lengthy excerpt from a document produced by the United States Commission on Civil Rights. It analyzes problems with many basic needs—housing, employment, health, safety, and education—currently unmet on many reservations.

STEREOTYPES OF NATIVE AMERICANS AND ALCOHOL

The following four documents all describe non-Native American views of Native Americans and alcohol. The first, from *The Jesuit Relations,* was written by French Jesuit priests who arrived in North America to serve as missionaries during the seventeenth century. Then an excerpt from a memoir written by an English man living in Wisconsin during the nineteenth century describes his view of Native American behavior after they receive their government payments. The next document is a short story wherein a young girl saves a Native American who has passed out from drinking too much; he changes his life as a result. The final document is a newspaper article published in 2003 as a result of a public survey regarding opinions surrounding alcohol in Gallup, New Mexico. These documents all describe drinking Native Americans in more bluntly stereotypic terms than occur in *Ceremony,* yet the attitudes found here are nevertheless all present, implicitly or explicitly, in the novel.

Early Jesuit Interactions with Native Americans

Jesuit priests, primarily from France, served as missionaries to Native Americans in northeast North America analogously to the Franciscan priests who served as missionaries in the Southwest. They kept extensive records of their experiences, composed from 1632–1673, records that have been compiled and translated into English. These records were originally intended to be simply communication between the mission in Quebec and the Jesuit superior in Paris. Some of the records address practical matters, while others describe more philosophical observations. These missionaries interacted most extensively with the Huron, primarily because French traders depended on the Huron for pelts, but the Jesuits also write of the Iroquois, Algonquins, and other tribes.

In this excerpt, a priest records the changes that have occurred among the "savages" once alcohol has been prohibited to them. The author describes the behavior of drunk Native Americans, who would exchange valuable beaver pelts for liquor rather than for food for their families; some of the Native Americans are so desperate for liquor that they trade in their own children. The priests are most concerned about the disorderly behavior because it impedes their religious work—they can't say mass and baptize converts who are chronically drunk. They solve their problem by punishing those who sell liquor to the Native Americans—not by throwing the traders into jail, as will be threatened later by the United States government, but by excommunicating them from the church. Excommunication means that a person does not have access to the sacraments and hence will not be able to go to heaven. According to this excerpt, the threat of excommunication worked, and the Native Americans became increasingly sober. Once sober, they took religious instruction from the priests. *Ceremony* demonstrates, however, that sobriety can be a necessary condition of religious experience generally, not only Christian ones. Tayo is the only character among his peers who is healed by the end of the novel; he is also the only one who begins to prefer sobriety.

FROM REUBEN GOLD THWAITES, ED., *THE JESUIT RELATIONS AND ALLIED DOCUMENTS,* VOL. 46

(The Burrows Co., 1899)

One of the most remarkable occurrences in Canada since the coming of Monseigneur the Bishop of Petraea, one which can be considered no less than marvelous, is the almost total suppression of drunkenness among our Savages. God has so blessed this good Prelate's zeal that he has at length overcome an evil which had been gaining in strength for so long a time, and which seemed beyond remedy.

Those who have mingled somewhat with the Savages (I speak only of those living near our settlements) are well aware that drink is a demon that robs them of their reason, and so inflames their passion that, after returning from the chase richly laden with beaver-skins, instead of furnishing their families with provisions, clothing, and other necessary supplies, they drink away the entire proceeds in one day and are forced to pass the winter in nakedness, famine, and all sorts of deprivation. There have been some whose mania was so extraordinary that, after stripping themselves of everything for liquor, they sold even their own children to obtain the means of intoxication. Children, too, when they are overcome with drink, beat their parents without being punished for it; Young men use it as a philter, corrupting the girls after making them drunk; those that have any quarrels pretend to be intoxicated, in order to wreak vengeance with impunity. Every night is filled with clamors, brawls, and fatal accidents, which the intoxicated cause in the cabins. Everything is permitted them, for they give as a satisfactory excuse that they were bereft of reason at the time; hence one cannot conceive the disorders which this diabolical vice has caused in this new Church. We found neither a time to instruct them, nor means to inspire them with horror of this sin; for they were always in a state of intoxication or of beggary—that is, either incapable of listening, or constrained to go in quest of food in the woods. This condition deeply moved the heart of Monseigneur of Petraea, who, seeing the fortunes of this new Christendom in danger of ruin, unless these evils were abolished, turned all his attention toward finding a remedy for the evil which had until then seemed incurable. And he happily found one; for, after the King's orders and the Governors' decrees had proved ineffectual, he, by excommunicating all the French who should give intoxicating liquors to the Savages, suppressed all these disorders, and they have not broken out again since the excommunication, so richly has it received Heaven's blessing. This result so surprised our better and more discreet Savages, that they came expressly to thank Monseigneur of Petraea on behalf of their entire Nation, acknowledging to him that they could not sufficiently admire the power of his Word, which had accomplished in a moment what had been so long attempted in vain.

The Father who has charge of the Tadoussac Mission, after witnessing in person the benefit to his Neophytes wrought by thus cutting off the supply of liquor, and after recording with joy the ease wherewith they can now be instructed, relates in addition a very signal act of Providence toward an aged Algonkin of seventy years. This man had formerly received instruction in our faith, but only cursorily; and had since then led a wandering life in the forests, without taking the trouble to apply for Baptism. At last, a mortal illness, which had afflicted him for a whole month, opened his eyes, and made him determine to go at the earliest possible moment in search of a Father to baptize him, promising himself that this resolve would restore his health. In very truth, it was restored contrary to his relatives' expectation; and he, having found the Father above Tadoussac, did not leave him until the latter had completed his instruction and had then conferred upon him this Sacrament, so earnestly desired. After that, he went back contented, and with the determination, after seventy years of Savage life, to pass the rest of his days as a good Christian. Those are signs of predestination—tardy, indeed, but of very good augury. (103–5)

An English Man's Observations

This next document is from a travel narrative originally published in London in 1842. The author wrote anonymously, and his identity has never been established. Before reaching Wisconsin, he had traveled through Canada, New York, and Michigan. The payment referred to in the excerpt is made by the United States government in exchange for land that had been ceded from the Menomenee tribe. The traders had previously agreed not to sell any Native Americans whiskey until after the government payment had occurred. In part, this text is comical, as the author presents those charged with enforcing the agreement as being too attracted to the whiskey themselves. They can't confiscate whiskey and stay sober simultaneously. Some of the author's attitude is founded in class differences; he perceives himself as superior to the people he is describing. Even in the end he intends to be amusing—he reveals his own fear but then redirects attention to the Native American who was so drunk he couldn't attack the author. Yet other details border on tragic, the uncared-for children crawling around in the lodge who evoke the children in the Gallup section of *Ceremony*. Throughout this excerpt, the author's descriptions of and vocabulary for Native Americans remains stereotypic. They are "savages" and "half-breeds." Everyone becomes drunken and dirty; they can't control—or don't see the benefit of controlling—the amount they drink. Only the author and his host remain sober and reasonable.

FROM *A MERRY BRITON IN PIONEER WISCONSIN*

(The State Historical Society of Wisconsin, 1950)

A negro barber from the Bay has been detected selling whisky to the Indians; in his lodge he had several barrels of whisky concealed, and the appointed mixed force of traders and sage Indians, who have endeavoured most laudably to keep the peace, and prevent the sale of whisky, have seized upon this [negro's] illicit store of the baneful fire-water, and the barrels having been rolled up in front of the Council Lodge, the agent and Osh Cosh are called on to decide as to its fate. Meantime the [negro] goes about exciting the pestilent half-breeds and profligate Indians to rescue his whisky, using the most abusive and indecent language, saying he will get up a big fight for his whisky, wishing he had his bowie knife, and, in short, provoking some hardy pioneer to thrash him.

During this afternoon, several seizures of whisky were made in the bush, and rolled up to the Council Lodge by the gallant band of Wolf River rangers; but alas for poor human nature! The band of whisky seekers were not proof against temptation, and in the midst of their seizures they could not help tasting, and from tasting went on to swigging, from swigging to tippling, and at last they cut a most ludicrous figure, marching about from lodge to lodge, and from tent to shanty, in quest of whisky, inveighing against the fire-water, while they were hardly able to stand; indeed, the major who commanded seemed to think he commanded a regiment, instead of a dozen boosy traders in red and grey night-caps, and some half-dozen old Indians in blankets; he carried his cudgel like a pike; "It looks well, at least, said my uncle Toby." Frequently halting his men in front of the Council Lodge, he would inspect them with great severity, give them speeches upon military discipline, read what he called the order of the day, which was the old declaration of independence; then putting himself at their head, march round the whisky barrels as if they were the trophies or spoils of war, followed by a mob of drunken half-breeds and whooping Indians. But at last the whisky was given up, and I saw the poor major, flat as a flounder, his occupation gone, his band dispersed, and in a hoarse voice he exclaimed against the ingratitude of the traders, who had not rewarded him for his zeal, even with a letter of thanks; "and after all I have gone through," said he, "I feel as if I had been beaten through hell with a soot-bag"; a singular, though not very elegant phrase for a man of his rank and standing to sport, even in the "Striped Apron."

The moment the last dollar was paid, down went the American flag, and the agent and his men rushed to their boat, plied their oars, and sheered off from the scene of action. Then the whisky sellers took the field. The young Indians clubbed together, and bought barrels of fire water, knocked in their heads with their clubs and tomahawks, and helped their friends all round to bowls and cups of the spirit, above proof—real firewater.

The result may be anticipated: the whole village became a scene of riot and debauchery. I retreated to my friendly trader's lodge, and found him expostulating with a few young Indians, upon the folly and wickedness of getting drunk. Indeed, this good man's words and example seemed to have considerable effect on his hearers; he begged of them to quit the village, bag and baggage, now they were paid. Several followed his advice at once, and others began to remove the mats &c. from their lodges; while the Indians who lived in his vicinity lodged their money for safe keeping in his hands. One old trapper actually deposited forty dollars with him, but would not go home—no, he preferred plunging into the midst of the riot and revelry. Next morning I hardly knew him, as he sneaked up, all covered with dirt and blood, to ask for his bundle.

That evening the rain came down in torrents; my host stood at the door of his lodge, and endeavoured to prevail on the Indians to pass on, and go home, but their drunken friends soon found them out. They came with kettles and cans full of whisky, which they insisted we should taste. My host obstinately refused, and loudly bawled, "Caun whisky, caun Ishcodaywa, bo"; and the result was, that a good deal of whisky was spilled, the Indians forcing cans against our lips, while we evaded the torrent; this was the most disagreeable part of the entertainment.

At night we barricaded the door with empty barrels and logs, but the Indians still came begging for money to buy more whisky, and the rain entered the roof and sides of our lodge. My blanket was saturated; and at midnight I sat up, finding it impossible to close an eye amidst the wild howling, terrific shouts, screams, love and war songs of the drunken savages without. I never heard, or hope to hear, anything half so horrible again. Indeed, as my host observed, it was worse than bedlam broke loose, it was like hell upon earth. Crowds of unhappy children crawled round our own lodge, crying bitterly; some of them contrived to creep into the empty barrels at our door, and that barrier was broken down, before morning, with a loud crash.

I had been trying to dose in a dry corner, when, looking up, I saw the tall spectral figure of a naked Indian leap through the door-way; he waved a glowing faggot in his hand, and shewed his wild distorted features covered with blood and dirt. "Now is the hour," thought I, "that my ramblings will have a finale, for *certes* this mad savage is on the eve of hurling the glowing log upon my devoted head"; but hardly had the thought flashed through my brain, when the savage fell prostrate on the floor, where, with a dozen more, we found him stark and gory, snoring away the effects of his last night's debauch. (93–99)

A Short Story in Which a White Girl Saves a Grown Native American

The following short story was originally published in a children's magazine. At the time the story was published, Michigan would have still been considered pioneer territory. Obviously, the plot is not entirely plausible. One overriding theme of the story is that Native Americans need white people to save them from their own weaknesses—even a white child is more advanced than an adult Native American. Notice the Native American's use of language, which more closely resembles the syntax of a small child than of a second-language speaker. Even given this theme, however, the stereotypes that abound are unnecessary. The author could have chosen to have Emily save the Native American (notice that he remains unnamed throughout, as if he is generic) from a bear due to any number of circumstances; the circumstance she chooses is the stereotype of the drunk Native American, the same stereotype several of the characters in *Ceremony* use to identify themselves. This Native American is so drunk, in fact, that he passes out and doesn't even awaken when a bear snuffles around him. By asserting herself, taking independent action, and shooting the bear (killing him with a single shot!), Emily seems to break out of gendered stereotypes—but immediately afterward she faints, demonstrating that she is a suitable girl after all.

FROM MARTHA G., "THE GRATEFUL INDIAN"

(*Robert Merry's Museum*, August 1862)

Mr. Martin had left his native town in Massachusetts with his wife and one child, to make a new home in the wild woods of Northern Michigan. He settled in the heart of the forest, far from any village, and miles from the nearest white neighbor, and with a strong arm and resolute will began the conquest of the mighty trees that seemed to forbid the progress of civilization.

Ere long the ringing blows of his ax brought him visitors from a neighboring small tribe of Indians, who showed plainly that he was no welcome intruder upon their favorite hunting-grounds. But he felt no fear, for the Indians had learned to respect the white man's power, and they knew that any harm done to one of the settlers, would speedily bring punishment upon their tribe from the strong arm of the government. Besides this, Mr. Martin soon managed to secure their good-will by various trifling presents, and by always treating them justly and kindly.

Little Emily, who at first was terrified by the sight of their dusky faces, strange costume, and fierce demeanor, soon learned to confide in them, and by her artless simplicity won their hearts.

Several years passed along without any noteworthy incident, except that new settlers arrived, and the woods were rapidly being cleared before the tide of emigration.

All might have remained peaceful, but for the bad character of some of the settlers. Traders had come, bringing whisky, the bane of the white man, and the terrible foe of the Indian.

Very soon the peace of the settlement was disturbed by drunken brawls, in which the Indians were frequent participants.

On one occasion, the chief of the neighboring tribe visited the settlement, and a party of unfeeling wretches contrived to entice him into one of the groggeries, and after getting him beastly drunk, turned him out to make his way home as best he might. He wandered away into the forest, and stupefied with liquor, fell beside a stump, and was soon fast asleep.

It happened that Emily had gone out berrying that afternoon, and as she was returning she passed near the sleeping Indian. She was startled upon seeing him, but thinking some accident might have befallen him, she stopped to see if he were hurt. She was unable to awake him, and was about to turn away, when to her horror she saw, at but a little distance from her, a large, black bear. Her first impulse was to scream, but checking it, she started to run with all her might for her father's cottage, which was about a quarter of a mile distant. She had run but a little way when she thought of the poor Indian left behind without power to escape from the bear, if it should attack him. What could she do? She saw that the animal had not followed her, but she dared not return for fear of being devoured. After a moment's thought, she determined to seek her father, who was at work in the field, and call him to rescue the Indian.

She flew to the field where her father had been plowing, but he had gone to the house, leaving his faithful dog beside the team. He had also left his rifle, which he always carried with him to the field, and in an instant the brave girl resolved to return to the defense of the sleeping man. Seizing the rifle and calling the dog she started at once, and in a few moments came in sight of the place where she had left him. Horrible! there was the bear standing directly over the man, who was now completely in its power. But the dog had seen him, and in an instant he bounded forward to attack him. The bear gave a sharp growl, and advanced to meet him, but Emily had not stood idle. Her father had taught her to use the rifle, and though she knew the danger should she only wound the animal, she laid the barrel across a stump, took as deliberate aim as her trembling hands would allow, and fired, just as the dog was about to grapple with the bear. The ball sped truly, the animal rolled over dead, and the danger was passed; but the excitement had proved too much for Emily, and she fainted.

The report of the rifle aroused the Indian, he sprang to his feet, and seeing the bear, started to run from it. In doing so he caught sight of Emily, and seeing the rifle lying by her, at once the truth flashed upon him.

He caught her in his strong arms, to bear her to the house; but was soon met by her father who had heard the noise. While the Indian was telling what he knew of the occurrence, Emily revived, and on her way home related the whole. The Indian could say little, but his looks showed his gratitude. "Me never forget," said he, as he turned away, and was soon out of sight.

Nothing was seen of the chief for many months. Mr. Martin learned that he had been so ashamed of his drunkenness, that he had removed far away, and he expected never to see him again. But early one morning, there was a knock at the door, and the Indian entered. "Me no forget," said he, and beckoned Emily to follow him. What was her delight to see, standing near the door, a beautiful deer with its fawn, which the Indian had brought as a present to the brave girl who had saved his life at the risk of her own. He had tamed it so that it would follow him like a dog, and though at first it was shy of Emily, it soon learned to love her better than any one else. The Indian pointed to the beautiful animal, saying, "Me no forget, me no get drunk more," darted away into the forest, and was never seen again in the settlement. (33–35)

A Contemporary Survey Regarding Alcohol Use in Gallup, New Mexico

The following newspaper article results from a poll taken of residents of Gallup, New Mexico—the same Gallup that serves as one setting in *Ceremony*. Several questions are addressed: whether the city should prohibit the sale of alcohol and become a "dry" city; whether to allow sale of alcohol on Sundays; how to address a litter problem exacerbated by liquor bottles; and whether the city should permit the sale of alcohol on publicly owned recreational facilities. Residents who completed the survey did not simply answer "yes" or "no" to these questions, however, but also added comments—several of which expose stereotypic assumptions regarding Native Americans. Although Native Americans aren't the only people criticized in the article, they are the only people singled out due to their ethnicity. The Gallup revealed in this article seems remarkably similar to the Gallup described in *Ceremony*, despite the intervening half century.

BILL DONOVAN, "SURVEY SHOWS CITY ADMITS HUGE PROBLEM WITH DRUNKS"

(Gallup *Independent*, October 13, 2003)

It appears that about 95 percent of the city's residents think Gallup is facing a severe alcoholism problem and something needs to be done about it.

That was made evident in the preliminary results issued by city officials from a survey now being taken of city utility users.

As of Oct. 7, a total of 829 utility users had turned in surveys. The final results are expected to be released in about two weeks.

The preliminary results, however, show something that Mayor Bob Rosebrough has been saying for months: Gallup residents want stricter regulations to control alcohol abuse.

Most (604) want the city to take a middle course as opposed to those who want to prohibit the sale of alcohol altogether (150) or don't want the city to do anything (65).

Almost seven out of every 10 residents support the idea of banning the sale of alcohol in glass containers because of the litter problem and feel that a deposit on glass beer and wine containers would alleviate the trash problem.

There was also a wide sentiment against the sale of alcohol at the city-owned golf course (542–284), Red Rock State Park (505–305) and on any city property during special events (518–289).

But residents seem to feel that sale of alcohol on a Sunday during a meal while watching pro football isn't too bad. That's winning right now by a 442–401 vote.

As for the city filing nuisance suits against bars that continue to be a problem, city residents are saying go for it by a vote of 665–143.

Here are some of the comments that people sent in with their surveys:

- Station security guards on the parking lots of supermarkets and at TradeMart package liquor. I've seen a lot of drunks walking, crossing the street from the store to the woods where they drink.

- Do not destroy economic development—tourism, etc.—by eliminating alcohol.

- Lock up the alcohol abusers in a tent city work camp.

- This is a real problem between Shop-n-Save and El Dorado Package Store. That area is an embarrassment to the whole city.

- You have the wrong solutions and proposals. You should try to target the reason why natives over drink. Try to look into their lives.

- When I lived in Iowa, they implemented this deposit and it reduced littering tremendously.

- Garden Deluxe and Tokay have no social value! (They) should be taxed heavily or outlawed.

- With the worst drinking problem around, the sacrifice of human lives for a dollar is absolutely insane. We endorse seat belts because it saves lives and sell booze that kills people.

- Downtown bars should be shut down. But allow restaurants to serve alcohol by the drink with a meal. You don't see beer cans lying around because there is a recycling center. Have a glass recycling center and the drunks will clean up their own mess.

- The chapter houses and the Navajo (Nation) Social Services (Division) should take a more aggressive role to help the city of Gallup control chronic public drunkenness.

- Since 80 percent of the street drunks are Native American, why not get together with the Navajo and Zuni tribes and detain these people at some point for five days or so.

- The majority of the drinkers that cause problems are not so much addicted to substances as they are lazy bums. Put them to work. They don't have to work in jail. Jail only rests them for the next tour of bumming.

- Alcohol should not be sold before noon and bars should not be allowed to open before noon.

- You don't see drunk Indians playing golf. That is why we can't get chain franchises like Chili's here. We need to get rid of these drunks.

- We seem to cater to the people with drinking problems instead of making them responsible for their actions. Behind our store, there are thousands of bottles that we pick up and dispose of. No one cares.

- Seeing drunks staggering around town and passed out in public places scares our children and implies to them that we adults find this behavior acceptable. It is imperative to the youth of our community that we take every step possible to change this.

- Prohibit any Native American from buying alcohol in Gallup. Let them buy it on the reservation. The Indians would have to legalize alcohol but they seem to want it bad enough they could get it approved.

- Gallup is unlivable. Do something.

- The city of Gallup should not infringe on the rights of citizens because of drunks. Instead, the city should invest in more and better trained public officials and should take domestic violence related to alcohol more seriously.

- How about getting rid of a couple of the judges who routinely hand out light sentences to repeat offender drunk drivers. We are being way too lenient!

- The American Bar should be closed! What a shame for the tourists to be subjected to such disgusting views of drunkenness and begging for money.

- In addition, smoking should be banned at all restaurants. Make McKinley County a DRY county!

A LAW PROHIBITING THE SALE OF ALCOHOL
TO NATIVE AMERICANS

The following document specifies punishments that could be meted out to anyone who sold liquor to Native Americans on the frontier. In denying alcohol to Native Americans, the government had a number of motives, including paternalistic ones—the government would function as a parent for those who couldn't, in its view, adequately care for themselves. Although this act applied only to Native Americans, the temperance movement through the United States was gaining strength, and many Americans believed that alcohol should be entirely prohibited to all people. This view eventually gained sufficient support for the passage of the Eighteenth Amendment to the Constitution in 1919, but Prohibition would last only a few years, until the Twenty-first Amendment repealing Prohibition was passed in 1933.

According to the law excerpted below, however, traders who sold alcohol to Native Americans could be punished with prison terms and fines, but few judges actually applied such sentences. The law also states that the liquor could be destroyed, presumably by dumping it out onto the ground, but the law does not stipulate that such action must occur, and it seldom did. The law exempts the War Department in order to allow soldiers access to liquor. At the end of the act, the legislature specifically states that Native Americans should be lawful witnesses under this law because ordinarily they were not.

FROM AN ACT TO AMEND AN ACT ENTITLED "AN ACT TO
REGULATE TRADE AND INTERCOURSE WITH THE
INDIAN TRIBES, AND TO PRESERVE PEACE ON THE
FRONTIERS," APPROVED JUNE THIRTIETH, EIGHTEEN
HUNDRED AND THIRTY-FOUR. THIRTY-SEVENTH
CONGRESS. SESS. II, CH. 24, FEBRUARY 13, 1862

Be it enacted by the Senate and House of Representatives of the United States of America in Congress assembled, That the twentieth section of the "Act to regulate trade and intercourse with the Indian tribes, and to preserve peace on the frontiers," approved June thirtieth, eighteen hundred and thirty-four, be, and the same is hereby, amended so as to read as follows, to wit:—

"Sec. 20. *And be it further enacted,* That if any person shall sell, exchange, give, barter, or dispose of any spirituous liquor or wine to any Indian under the charge of any Indian superintendent or Indian agent appointed by the United States, or shall introduce or attempt to introduce any spirituous liquor or wine into the Indian country, such person, on conviction thereof before the proper district court of the United States, shall be imprisoned for a period not exceeding two years, and shall be fined not more than three hundred dollars: *Provided, however,* That it shall be a sufficient defence to any charge of introducing or attempting to introduce liquor into the Indian country if it be proved to be done by order of the War Department, or of any officer duly authorized thereto by the War Department. And if any superintendent of Indian affairs, Indian agent or sub-agent, or commanding officer of a military post, has reason to suspect or is informed that any white person or Indian is about to introduce or has introduced any spirituous liquor or wine into the Indian country, in violation of the provisions of this section, it shall be lawful for such superintendent, agent, sub-agent, or commanding officer, to cause the boats, stores, packages, wagons, sleds, and places of deposit of such person to be searched; and if any such liquor is found therein, the same, together with the boats, teams, wagons, and sleds used in conveying the same, and also the goods, packages, and peltries of such person, shall be seized and delivered to the proper officer, and shall be proceeded against by libel in the proper court, and forfeited, one half to the informer and the other half to the use of the United States; and if such person be a trader, his license shall be revoked and his bond put in suit. And it shall moreover be lawful for any person in the service of the United States, or for any Indian, to take and destroy any ardent spirits or wine found in the Indian country, except such as may be introduced therein by the War Department. And in all cases arising under this act Indians shall be competent witnesses."

Approved, February 13, 1862.

PERSONAL ACCOUNTS OF NATIVE AMERICANS AND ALCOHOL PROBLEMS

The next three documents illustrate how devastating alcohol addictions can be, both to alcoholics themselves and to others. All three describe specific moments of tension between individual Native Americans and alcohol. The first excerpt comes from a biography of Ira Hayes, a Pima from the Gila River Reservation who served in the U.S. Marines during World War II. After his return, his alcoholism frequently led to trouble with the law. The next excerpt is taken from a memoir by Michael Dorris, who adopted a boy named Adam. After years of struggling with Adam's various disabilities, Dorris realized his son suffered from FAS. The final excerpt is a table listing results of a survey regarding alcohol and other drug use among contemporary Native American high school students.

The Experience of Ira Hayes

Because of his experience fighting in the Pacific during World War II, Ira Hayes returned to the United States as a hero. He had fought in the battle of Iwo Jima, and he is one of the men raising the American flag in the famous photograph illustrating the allied victory; this photograph is among the most famous taken during the war. Although Hayes felt more comfortable among his military buddies than he did in a public role, the popularity of that photograph brought him much public recognition. For this and other reasons, he began drinking heavily after his return to the United States. He lost jobs because of his drinking and was repeatedly arrested, as the excerpt illustrates. Ten years after the war ended, Hayes died after a night of drinking, frozen from the January cold. One can easily imagine some of the characters in *Ceremony* ending up in similar circumstances, even Tayo had he not participated in his ceremony.

FROM ALBERT HEMINGWAY, *IRA HAYES: PIMA MARINE*

(University Press of America, 1988)

[Ira Hayes] began going to Phoenix. Someone would recognize him and offer to buy the "hero" a drink. Not wanting to offend anyone, he accepted. He got drunk. It would be the first of many times.

The arrests started to mount. . . . Ira tried desperately to overcome his growing dependency on alcohol. Through a friend, a Creek Indian, he got a job at a warehouse in Phoenix and slept on a cot in a rear room of the building. The two would have dinner together and Ira would reminisce about his war experiences and remember his "old buddies." They made an agreement with each other: if Ira developed an urge to take a drink, he would call and they would get together and talk. On such occasions, Ira would telephone and the two would have long conversations into the night. It seemed to be working and each hoped it was the beginning to his recovery. Then one evening Ira's friend wasn't home. The temptation proved to be too great. The next morning, he was back in jail.

As the demands on Ira began to mount, so did his drinking....
    Then tragedy struck. He was found wandering, dazed, shoeless, and incoherent on a Chicago street. He was pictured in the *Chicago Sun-Times,* sad and dejected. The photographers didn't even allow him to wash his face.

Not having the twenty-five dollars for the fine imposed on him, Hayes was sentenced to seventeen days in jail. He was fired from his job.... Eventually, the *Chicago Sun-Times* intervened in his behalf and bailed him out. A "rehabilitation fund" was established in his name to get "the hero on his feet." The story ran in every major paper in the country. It was the height of humiliation. (150–53)

Adam Dorris and Fetal Alcohol Syndrome

In publishing *The Broken Cord,* Michael Dorris brought the issue of FAS to public attention more effectively than doctors and scientists could have. His book tells the story of his adoption of Adam (and later, additional children), initially as a single father. Adam was obviously developmentally delayed, but Dorris believed that he would make rapid progress once he was in a stable environment. Such progress never occurred. Initially, the configuration of Adam's disabilities puzzled Dorris and others, since they didn't seem limited to one area. Eventually, through research and personal observation, Dorris realized that his son suffered from FAS, and that regardless of efforts to compensate for his disabilities, Adam would never acquire many basic skills. Much of *The Broken Cord* addresses FAS, especially as it affects Native American populations, as Dorris alternates between telling his own family's story and exploring the more wide-ranging implications of this condition. This excerpt describes the frustrating nature of Adam's learning disability. Because he is unable to think abstractly, and particularly unable to see relationships between cause and effect, all kinds of other learning are impossible—even types of learning that can seem more like common sense. This aspect of Adam's disability is most discouraging to Dorris, who understands how the imagination is so fundamentally human.

FROM MICHAEL DORRIS, *THE BROKEN CORD*

(HarperPerennial, 1989)

[Adam] did not learn from his mistakes, inconveniently maddening as they often were. He clung to established order with tenacity, refusing to adapt to fluctuations in his external environment. If he had successfully worn a T-shirt and no coat in the summer, then by golly, he'd slip from the house in identical clothing in January, even though the temperature was well below zero. When he learned a new skill, he would more often than not focus on some extraneous detail within the overall structure, and drop anchor. The whole constellation of actions, the essential mixed with the accidental would become entrenched, and no single part could be selectively jettisoned. There were no gradations, no interchangeable parts to a pattern once he embraced it. Right clothes = T-shirt. Period.

But his greatest problem... was his lack of a particular kind of imagination. He could not, cannot, project himself into the future: "If I do *x*, then *y* (good or bad) will follow." His estimation of consequences was so hazy that it translated into an approach to action so conservative that it appeared to be stubborn....

...If left to monitor his own medication, he might take all three of a day's doses at once in order to "get them over with" or might sequester them in a drawer "so that I won't run out." He might take a dollar bill out of my wallet, even when he had ten of his own, "because I wanted to save mine." The question "why" has never had much meaning for Adam; the kind of cause-effect relationship it implies does not compute for him. (200–201)

Alcohol and Other Drug Use Among Native American High School Students

The table below illustrates the results of a survey administered to students attending high schools funded by the BIA in 2001. A total of 5,654 students from 66 high schools participated in the survey, representing slightly over 60 percent of all eligible students. The table breaks down alcohol and drug use by type of drug, gender, and academic grade of user. It distinguishes between those students who have tried alcohol or other drugs, perhaps only once, and those who use alcohol and/or other drugs regularly. Even among ninth graders, the rate of alcohol and marijuana use is high; a significant majority have tried both. Even cocaine, considered a much more potent—and addictive—drug, has been used by nearly one-fifth of ninth graders and over a quarter of twelfth graders. The distinctions between male and female use of all the drugs is minimal, with the most significant differences only about four percentage points.

These statistics support the realism of *Ceremony,* wherein both male and female characters drink excessively, although the contexts of male drinking are different from the contexts of female drinking. Such high drug and alcohol use among females is particularly disturbing when one considers the already high rate of FAS among Native Americans.

FROM "TOBACCO, ALCOHOL, AND OTHER DRUG USE
AMONG HIGH SCHOOL STUDENTS IN BUREAU OF INDIAN
AFFAIR-FUNDED SCHOOLS—UNITED STATES, 2001"

(*Morbidity and Mortality Weekly Report,* Center for Disease Control,
November 7, 2003)

Percentage of High School Students at Schools Funded by the Bureau of Indian Affairs (BIA) Who Reported Alcohol and/or Drug Use, by Sex and Grade

Characteristic	% lifetime alcohol use*	% current alcohol use†	% episodic heavy drinking‡	% lifetime marijuana use§	% current marijuana use	% current inhalant use††	% lifetime cocaine use‡‡	% lifetime methamphetamine use§§
Sex								
Female	82.9	46.8	36.6	77.2	47.7	4.9	21.6	21.4
Male	78.3	50.9	40.3	76.8	51.6	5.1	21.1	19.0
Grade								
9	75.0	45.4	36.0	73.6	51.5	6.3	18.2	18.0
10	80.5	48.1	39.0	75.7	49.2	4.7	20.2	19.7
11	84.4	51.5	39.1	79.5	50.0	4.4	23.3	19.6
12	86.9	52.8	41.7	81.8	46.4	3.5	26.5	25.4
Total	80.6	48.8	38.4	77.0	49.7	5.0	21.3	20.2

*Ever had one or more drinks of alcohol
†Drank alcohol on ≥1 of the 30 days preceding the survey
‡Drank five or more drinks of alcohol on one occasion on ≥1 of the 30 days preceding the survey
§Ever used marijuana
**Used marijuana on ≥1 of the 30 days preceding the survey
††Sniffed glue or breathed the contents of aerosol spray cans or inhaled any paints or sprays to become intoxicated on ≥1 of the 30 days preceding the survey
‡‡Ever tried any form of cocaine (e.g., powder, "crack," or "freebase")
§§Ever used methamphetamines (also called "speed," "crystal," "crank," or "ice")
Source: BIA Youth Risk Survey, United States, 2001

NATIVE AMERICANS AS BRAND NAMES

The next document is an excerpt from a verdict of a court case brought by the Hornell Brewing Company, which manufactured "Crazy Horse Malt Liquor." Responding to objections by Native Americans and others to that name, Congress had passed a law forbidding the use of the name "Crazy Horse" for such a product. The brewing company sued on the basis of their right to free speech. The judge who wrote the verdict agreed with the plaintiff, supporting free speech even, or especially, when it is offensive. Native Americans were particularly incensed over the adoption of the brand name "Crazy Horse" because the historical Chief Crazy Horse had strongly discouraged alcohol use. It might seem odd that a brand of alcohol would be named after a person who preached temperance, but the employees of the Hornell Brewing Company may well have been acting out of ignorance, relying on the stereotype of the drunken Native American rather than any actual knowledge of Chief Crazy Horse. The judge suggests that rather than permit government censorship, a more appropriate response to offensive commercial speech in a democracy is to organize a boycott of the product; if the corporation cannot make money from a product, the corporation will quickly discontinue the product's manufacture.

FROM *HORNELL BREWING CO., INC. AND DON VULTAGGIO, PLAINTIFFS, V. NICHOLAS BRADY*, AS UNITED STATES SECRETARY FOR THE DEPARTMENT OF THE TREASURY; THE UNITED STATES DEPARTMENT OF THE TREASURY; STEPHEN E. HIGGINS, AS DIRECTOR OF THE BUREAU OF ALCOHOL, TOBACCO & FIREARMS; AND WILLIAM T. EARLE, AS CHIEF, INDUSTRY COMPLIANCE DIVISION FOR THE BUREAU OF ALCOHOL, TOBACCO & FIREARMS, DEFENDANTS. UNITED STATES DISTRICT COURT FOR THE EASTERN DISTRICT OF NEW YORK
819 F. SUPP. 1227; 1993 U.S. DIST. LEXIS 4662

FEBRUARY 5, 1993, DECIDED

The matter was fully briefed and oral argument was heard on January 27, 1993. For the reasons set forth below, the undersigned respectfully recommends that summary judgment be granted in favor of plaintiffs on the First Amendment claim, and in favor of defendants on the five remaining claims.

Background and Facts

The following facts are undisputed unless otherwise indicated. Plaintiff Hornell Brewing Company ("Hornell") is a New York corporation which maintains its principal place of business in Brooklyn, New York and produces and markets alcoholic and non-alcoholic beverages including "The Original Crazy Horse Malt Liquor" ("Crazy Horse"). Plaintiff Don Vultaggio is Chairman and co-owner of Hornell. In February, 1992, the Bureau of Alcohol, Tobacco, and Firearms ("BATF") issued a Certificate of Label approval ("COLA") to Hornell's bottler, G. Heileman Brewing Company ("GHBC"), authorizing the bottling and distribution of the Crazy Horse product. The certification process of BATF includes the consideration of whether the label is misleading, fraudulent, or obscene. Hornell introduced Crazy Horse in fourteen states in March 1992. To date, Crazy Horse is distributed in thirty-one states through over 200 wholesalers who resell to over 100,000 retailers. Hornell claims that Crazy Horse Malt Liquor was to be the first product in a series of Hornell beverages that celebrate the American West.

The introduction of the product caused a surge of indignation throughout Congress, seemingly initiated by the United States Surgeon General Antonia Novello. In April 1992, Dr. Novello held a press conference in Rapid City, South Dakota, where she criticized the choice of the name Crazy Horse for a malt liquor. She accused Hornell of "insensitive and malicious marketing" and encouraged the leaders of Indian nations to use public outrage to force Crazy Horse off the market. Subsequently, members of Congress joined the effort to prohibit use of the name Crazy Horse on the malt liquor product. By letter dated April 20, 1992, South Dakota senator Larry Pressler directed Hornell to change the product's name or donate its proceeds to Native American causes because "defamation of this hero is an insult to Indian culture." Similarly, on April 27, 1992, Senator Tom Daschle wrote to Hornell expressing his displeasure with the use of the name Crazy Horse. On May 19, 1992, Dr. Novello appeared before the House Select Committee on Children, Youth and Family. Representative Patricia Schroeder had called the hearing to consider legislation to prohibit use of the name Crazy Horse on alcoholic beverages. No representative of Hornell was permitted to appear at the hearing.

Subsequently, Representative Frank Wolf offered an amendment to the Treasury, Postal Service and General Government Appropriations Bill then under consideration. The amendment would have prohibited the use of trade names or brand names for alcoholic beverages that bore the name of any deceased individual of public prominence if the use of the name were likely to degrade or disparage the reputation of the individual. Representative Wolf made clear that the introduction of the Crazy Horse product was the impetus for the proposed amendment, stating, "The language has been put in because this brewer has developed an alcoholic beverage called Crazy Horse. Crazy Horse was an Indian Chief who was known for urging his people not to drink alcohol." A Point of Order was sustained because the amendment attempted to create legislation through an appropriations bill in violation of House of Representatives rules. Wolf then proposed an amendment explicitly aimed at prohibiting the use of the name "Crazy Horse" on any alcoholic beverage. The House approved this bill and referred it to the Conference Committee. Rather than adopting the House bill, the Senate Committee adopted a resolution directing Hornell to negotiate with Sioux leaders and enter into a binding agreement abandoning the use of Crazy Horse as a brand name to "obviate the need for legislation."

Hornell claims in its moving papers that Hornell representatives met with Sioux leaders to negotiate a resolution. Hornell sought to protect its investment, distributors, suppliers, and work force, in the discontinuation of the Crazy Horse product. Hornell claims that the Sioux insisted on a general ban of Native American names and symbols in connection with the sale of all commercial products and services. Because this demand was beyond the scope of Hornell's authority, negotiations were terminated.

Senators Daschle and Adams then proposed legislation banning use of the name Crazy Horse on alcoholic products. Senator Adams explicitly rebuked Hornell in his statement to the Senate, stating that Hornell had been "insensitive and disrespectful" to the Sioux's request that Hornell discontinue Crazy Horse Malt Liquor. The statute was enacted on October 1, 1992 and reads as follows:

> Upon the date of enactment of this Act, the Bureau of Alcohol, Tobacco, and Firearms (ATF) shall deny any application for a certificate of label approval, including a certificate of label approval already issued, which authorizes the use of the name Crazy Horse on any distilled spirit, wine, or malt beverage product; Provided, that no funds appropriated under this Act or any other Act shall be expended by ATF for enforcement of this section and regulations thereunder, as it related to malt beverage glass bottles to which labels have been permanently affixed by means of painting and heat treatment, which were ordered on or before September 15, 1992, or which are owned for resale by wholesalers or retailers.

On November 17, 1992, defendant William T. Earle, Chief of the Industry Compliance Division of BATF issued a letter to G. Heileman Brewing Company ("GHBC"), which bottles Crazy Horse Malt Liquor for Hornell, stating that Public Law 102–393, § 633 "mandates the denial of labels [for Crazy Horse Malt Liquor] which have already been approved" and that "BATF is required to 'deny any application for a certificate of label approval, including a certificate of label approval already issued, which authorizes the use of the name Crazy Horse on any distilled spirit, wine, or malt beverage product.'"

Plaintiff filed its Complaint for declaratory and injunctive relief on December 4, 1992, and also moved the court for a preliminary injunction, preventing defendants from enforcing Public Law 102–393, § 633.

Discussion

B. First Amendment

The fundamental principle of the First Amendment is that the government may not prohibit speech because the ideas expressed therein are offensive.... When the government does regulate to prohibit speech based on its content, the regulation is presumptively invalid unless the speech falls into an unprotected category to which lesser standards apply.... Commercial speech is not considered unprotected, but it does enjoy a lesser degree of First Amendment protection than protected speech....

Plaintiffs claim that Public Law 102–393, § was enacted for the purpose of "protecting Native Americans from the offensive exploitation of a former Sioux leader's name."...It bears repeating that the desire to protect society or certain members of society from the purported offensiveness of particular speech is not a substantial interest which justifies its prohibition....

One of the basic premises of advertising is that if it is too offensive to too many people, its use will be counterproductive, for those who are offended will not only refuse to buy the product, but also, if they are sufficiently offended, they will attempt to persuade others to refuse also.

Conclusion

For the reasons stated above, it is respectfully recommended that summary judgment in favor of the plaintiff be granted on the basis that Public Law 102–393, § 633 violates the First Amendment of the Constitution.

Although this court has found that Public Law 102–393, § 633 violates the First Amendment for the reasons discussed above, this decision should not be read as either condoning or endorsing plaintiffs' choice of name for their product Crazy Horse Malt Liquor. The Court can well appreciate that the use of the name of a revered Native American leader, who preached sobriety and resisted exploitation under the hand of the United States government, is offensive and may be viewed as an exploitation of Native Americans throughout this country. The choice may be particularly insensitive given the ample documentation of alcohol abuse and its destructive results among Native Americans. Nevertheless, a price we pay in this country for ordered liberty is that we are often exposed to that which is offensive to some, perhaps even to many. It is from our exposure to all that is different that we best learn to address it, change it, and sometimes tolerate and appreciate it.... To those who are offended by the use of the Crazy Horse Malt Liquor label, the directive of the district court in Sambo's of Ohio, Inc. v. Toledo, 466 F. Supp. 177, 180 (N.D. Ohio 1979) is particularly apt:

If they are offended by the word [Crazy Horse] not only can they refuse to patronize the plaintiffs, but they, too, can erect signs, carry placards, or publish advertisements designed to persuade others to refuse to patronize the plaintiffs. That is what freedom of speech is all about. One cannot have freedom of speech for himself if it can be denied to others, nor is speech free if only innocuous utterances are permitted.... It would be selling our birthright for a mess of pottage to hold that because language is offensive and distasteful even to a majority of the public, a legislative body may forbid its use.

It is in this spirit that the undersigned respectfully recommends that Public Law 102–393, § 633 be declared an unconstitutional violation of the First Amendment.

John M. Azrack

United States Magistrate Judge

NATIVE AMERICAN BOARDING SCHOOLS

The next two documents discuss the controversial issue of the boarding schools that Native American children were required to attend during the late nineteenth century. The goal of the government in mandating such attendance was to "Americanize" Native Americans, that is, to convert them into Europeans culturally if not biologically. Students were required to wear European-style clothing and to speak English only. If they spoke their tribal languages, they would be severely punished. Upon arrival, they had their hair cut, a significant and demeaning symbolic gesture. They were generally taught trades but were not provided a liberal arts education—they were expected to earn their living from manual labor rather than join the professional class. The excerpt from Zitkala-Ša's memoir illustrates how unhappy she was when she arrived at her boarding school in Indiana. The next document, an editorial from the *New York Times,* reveals some of the controversy around the policy of forcibly removing children from their parents, even among people who agreed with the ultimate goal of assimilating Native Americans into mainstream American culture. The *Times* editorial suggests that permitting children to be educated on their own reservations might in the end prove more effective.

Zitkala-Ša's Experience

Zitkala-Ša was a Sioux born in 1876, as the "Indian wars" were drawing to a close. She attended boarding school in Indiana and eventually spent two years at Earlham College there. She was among the first Native Americans to publish articles and books that were comparatively free of white editorial intervention. Among her goals in composing her books was to capture her ancestral culture that she believed was disappearing. In this excerpt, she describes her arrival at boarding school and all of its strange practices. For example, because everyone wore shoes (rather than moccasins), the hallways were particularly loud as people walked through them. Zitkala-Ša was accustomed to maintaining a much quieter presence. She feels immodest in her European-style clothing, although her white teachers would have said that Native American clothing was immodest. In these statements, Zitkala-Ša clearly reveals how such concepts as "modesty" are dependent on a given cultural context for their definitions. She states that she felt her spirit break when her hair was cut; she lost, that is, her will to resist. In *Ceremony,* Old Betonie reveals that he had attended a similar school, though his motive expressly contradicted the motives of the school—he learned English not as a step in abandoning his culture, but in order to fulfill his traditional role.

FROM ZITKALA-ŠA, "THE SCHOOL DAYS OF AN INDIAN GIRL," *AMERICAN INDIAN STORIES*

(University of Nebraska Press, 1985)

The first day in the land of apples was a bitter-cold one; for the snow still covered the ground, and the trees were bare. A large bell rang for breakfast, its loud metallic voice crashing through the belfry overhead and into our sensitive ears. The annoying clatter of shoes on bare floors gave us no peace. The constant clash of harsh noises, with an undercurrent of many voices murmuring an unknown tongue, made a bedlam within which I was securely tied. And though my spirit tore itself in struggling for its lost freedom, all was useless.

A paleface woman, with white hair, came up after us. We were placed in a line of girls who were marching into the dining room. These were Indian girls, in stiff shoes and closely clinging dresses. The small girls wore sleeved aprons and shingled hair. As I walked noiselessly in my soft moccasins, I felt like sinking to the floor, for my blanket had been stripped from my shoulders. I looked hard at the Indian girls, who seemed not to care that they were even more immodestly dressed than I, in their tightly fitting clothes....

I watched my chance, and when no one noticed I disappeared. I crept up the stairs as quietly as I could in my squeaking shoes,—my moccasins had been exchanged for shoes.... I found a large room with three white beds in it.... On my hands and knees I crawled under the bed, and cuddled myself in the dark corner.

From my hiding place I peered out, shuddering with fear whenever I heard footsteps near by.... Women and girls entered the room.... I remember being dragged out, though I resisted by kicking and scratching wildly. In spite of myself, I was carried downstairs and tied fast in a chair.

I cried aloud, shaking my head all the while until I felt the cold blades of the scissors against my neck, and heard them gnaw off one of my thick braids. Then I lost my spirit. Since the day I was taken from my mother I had suffered extreme indignities. People had stared at me. I had been tossed about in the air like a wooden puppet. And now my long hair was shingled like a coward's! In my anguish I moaned for my mother, but no one came to comfort me. Not a soul reasoned quietly with me, as my own mother used to do; for now I was only one of many little animals driven by a herder. (52–56)

Boarding Schools Versus Reservation Schools

The following editorial discusses the conflict between parents who want their children to remain home with them on reservations and the government that desires to assimilate Native American children precisely by removing them from their traditional surroundings. The *Times* interprets the government's goal as laudable but suggests that the current policy may be impractical. Parents will provide much less resistance, the editorial implies, if their children are educated locally, even if they are educated according to white standards. Although the writer sympathizes with parents who miss their children, he does not therefore accept Native American cultures as equally valid to more mainstream American culture. The editorial assumes, in fact, that Native American cultures are inherently inferior to those derived from Europe. Assimilation is necessary—the question is how to accomplish it most effectively.

FROM "INDIAN EDUCATION"

(*New York Times,* Sept. 20, 1892)

A dispatch from Kingman, in Arizona, announces that a few days ago representatives from five tribes or bands of Indians met at Pine Springs to protest against having their children taken away and sent to Government schools in the East. It is said that some of them were for resorting to arms, and that a great many families had gone to the mountains to prevent their boys and girls from being carried off. It is quite possible that the parents have exaggerated the risks they run, but their feeling that it is a hardship to have their children carried a long distance away is natural. The Fifty-first Congress at its second session passed a law authorizing and directing the Commissioner of Indian Affairs "to make and enforce by proper means such rules and regulations as will secure the attendance of Indian children of suitable age and health at schools established and maintained for their benefit." This compulsory attendance law furnishes the basis for the action of which the Arizona bands complain. But whether Congress foresaw that the authority thus given would be used to take children against the will of their parents hundreds or thousands of miles from their homes may not be so clear. To civilized people such a removal will, of course, seem a great opportunity for the youngsters. They are cared for, fed, clothed, and instructed without cost, and are made much fitter for citizenship and for success in life than their companions who receive no such advantages. But while we understand all this, to the Indian fathers and mothers the forcible wresting away of their children must look very much like kidnapping.

There is no doubt that the main hope of civilizing the red men and of bringing them into line with American citizens lies in the training of their children. It would be unwise to allow the prejudices of ignorant parents to deprive the rising generation of the provisions made by the Government for their benefit. Yet it is quite evident that in this matter sound judgment and careful consideration of the peculiar circumstances of the red men are needed. Commissioner Morgan has noted that the Indians "are loath to have their children taken from them, even for a short time. They are devotedly attached to them, miss their companionship, and are accustomed to rely upon their assistance in the performance of such simple duties as they are capable of." Perhaps in this statement may be found an explanation of the feeling of bitterness against the Government which is now reported to exist among some of the Arizona bands. It would hardly be fair to charge them with prejudice against education if what they are really prejudiced against should turn out to be simply the sending of their offspring far away. It does not appear from the dispatch that they would object to having them instructed in schools where the parents could still have a share in their companionship. The problem, no doubt, is a difficult one, but it is evident that, while an admirable work is done by the Eastern training schools—one of whose great advantages is in taking the children at an impressionable age away from their savage home surroundings—yet the ultimate reliance for the great body of the Indians must be in schools on and near the reservations. Commissioner Morgan in his last report made a strong appeal to Congress for the multiplication of day schools, fully supplied with all means to make up for the lack of home instruction. It would require no very extravagant amount to furnish sufficient schools and instruction for such of the Indian children of school age as cannot now be accommodated somewhere, and it might be a wise expenditure to do this within the next few years. With more reservation schools the compulsory attendance law would be enforced with a better grace and without embittering the lives of Indian parents in seeking the benefit of their offspring.

NATIVE AMERICANS AND OTHER ISSUES OF
SOCIAL WELFARE

The final document is a lengthy excerpt from a report issued by the United States Commission on Civil Rights in 2003. It provides quantities of evidence that Native Americans have been vastly underserved by their government and society. By virtually every measure, their standard of living has been inferior to the average American's. They have been more likely to live in poverty, less likely to be well educated, more likely to die young, and less likely to receive adequate health care. The Commission sees each of these issues as related to inadequate funding from the federal government, and it urges better funding from both an ethical and legal perspective. The excerpt below addresses a range of basic needs, comparing the average Native American situation to the American population as a whole. Of course, statistics will vary dramatically from reservation to reservation—but so do statistics from one major city to another or between metropolitan and rural areas generally. The Commission supports its findings not only with quantifiable data like statistics but also provides descriptions of specific individual circumstances. The definition of "inadequate housing" becomes much more clear after one reads the description of one particular family's house. While this house might be an extreme example, the Commission implies that it is by no means unique. In *Ceremony,* Silko does not enumerate the economic pressures felt by every family; yet various scenes in the novel illustrate nearly every issue discussed in this excerpt.

FROM *A QUIET CRISIS: FEDERAL FUNDING AND UNMET NEEDS IN INDIAN COUNTRY,* BY THE U.S. COMMISSION ON CIVIL RIGHTS (2003)

Native Americans have a lower life expectancy—nearly six years less—and higher disease occurrence than other racial/ethnic groups. Roughly 13 percent of Native American deaths occur among those under the age of 25, a rate three times more than that of the total U.S. population. Native American youth are more than twice as likely to commit suicide, and nearly 70 percent of all suicidal acts in Indian Country involve alcohol. Native Americans are 670 percent more likely to die from alcoholism, 650 percent more likely to die from tuberculosis, 318 percent more likely to die from diabetes, and 204 percent more likely to suffer accidental death when compared with other groups. These disparities exist because of disproportionate poverty, poor education, cultural differences, and the absence of adequate health service delivery in most Native communities.

One of the largest barriers to adequate health care for Native Americans is *access.* Only 28 percent of Native Americans have private health insurance through an employer; 55 percent rely on the Indian Health Service (IHS) within HHS [Health and Human Services] for all their health care needs. According to the National Center for Health Statistics, Native Americans make fewer visits to physicians' offices and hospital outpatient departments than any other racial or ethnic group. In 1999, per 100,000 people, whites made 293 visits to the doctor, Asian Americans made 233 visits, blacks made 211 visits, and Native Americans made only 54. On the other hand, they made more emergency room visits than whites or Asian Americans. (34–35)

Contrasting Native Americans with other populations for whom the federal government has direct responsibility for health care—such as veterans, Medicaid recipients, and federal prison inmates—distinct disparities in expenditures are evident. In 2003, the government will spend nearly $6,000 for each Medicare recipient and more than $5,200 on each veteran who uses services of the Veterans Administration. Federal prisoners and Medicaid patients will each receive more than twice the amount spent on Native American health care ... in 2002, the Department of Defense spent $3,324 per military member using its services. Even after adding IHS medical and non-medical (such as community water and sewer) per person expenditures, IHS spends less on its service users than the government spends on any other group receiving public health care. This disparity in spending is amplified by the poorer health conditions of many in the Native American community and represents a direct affront to the legal and moral obligation the nation has to improve Indian health status. (43)

According to members of the Senate Indian Affairs Committee, roughly 90,000 Indian families are homeless or under-housed; more than 30 percent of reservation households are crowded; 18 percent are severely crowded; and one in five Indian houses lacks complete plumbing facilities. Roughly 16 percent of Native American homes are without telephones, while only 6 percent of non-Native households lack telephone service. Some Native American communities lack even the infrastructure for telephone installation, hampering basic communication. Overall, approximately 40 percent of on-reservation housing is considered inadequate as compared with roughly 6 percent nationwide.... Regional variations exist and are associated with geographic isolation, proximity to urban economies, and private ownership of land. For example, in Alaska, Arizona, and New Mexico, the rate of overcrowding and substandard housing is more than 60 percent.

Basic housing provisions that are taken for granted elsewhere in the nation are often absent on reservations. For example, fewer than 50 percent of homes on reservations are connected to a public sewer system. Twenty percent of homes must resort to other means of sewage disposal, often resulting in "honeybucket" methods in which household waste and sewage are collected into large receptacles that are later dumped into lagoons beyond the boundaries of the village or tribe. Settlements that use this system often suffer serious contamination and severe bacterial and viral infection from the waste and sewage washing back into the communities after heavy rainfall; this system also results in the poisoning of crops. (51)

The need for homelands and housing predates modern history and goes back to the removal and allotment eras. At that time, hundreds of millions of acres of land were surrendered by tribes, and Native peoples were forced to relocate to unfamiliar and undeveloped regions where they had to struggle to even build traditional Native housing structures. It was not until the Snyder Act of 1921 that the Bureau of Indian Affairs (BIA) in the Department of the Interior was given the authority to provide housing assistance on reservations, although the federal government was not swift to address many housing needs. The Housing Act of 1937 established the nation's intention to eliminate unsanitary and unsafe housing conditions for poor American families. However, again the needs of Native Americans were largely ignored, as the act was not initially interpreted to include them. The omission of Native Americans from the act reflected a post-World War II shift in federal policy away from self-determination and toward decreasing the federal trust responsibility. It was not until 1961 that the federal government began to substantially address the housing needs of non-urban Indians by redirecting the Housing Act to include Indian reservations. Thus, it took the federal government nearly 30 years to recognize the need for housing assistance on Native American lands despite long-documented evidence of treacherous living conditions. (52)

The Native American population faces circumstances, and hence needs, that differ from the general population. The dismal housing situation is compounded by the difficulties many Native Americans face in accessing credit and loans, due in part to their unique relationship with the federal government and the fact that they do not own land titles. Fewer than 33 percent of Native Americans own their own homes, compared with 67 percent of all Americans. In 1996, the government attempted to address these unique concerns, as well as housing conditions, with the passage of the Native American Housing Assistance and Self-Determination Act (NAHASDA). (53)

One reservation story illustrates the extreme overcrowding characteristic of many who reside on reservations. A one-bedroom house that was built in the 1960s as one of the first transitional low-income housing units on a Dakota plains reservation—and was abandoned in the 1970s because of extreme deterioration—is now regularly occupied by a family of 12 to 18 people. Housing advocates describe the deteriorating condition of the house:

> There is very little insulation in the house and the winds rip through it, even with plastic over the windows. In the winter, the single wood stove and the oven going full blast in the kitchen cannot keep the house warm. The roof over the bedroom is collapsing. Floors in the bedroom, kitchen, and front room are caving in. The electrical wiring is disintegrating. The bathroom fixtures spray water across the room.... Household residents believe the young children have recurring illnesses because of the extreme cold in the bedroom and on the front room floor where they often sleep. [Quoted from National American Indian Housing Council, *Too Few Rooms: Residential Crowding in Native American Communities and Alaska Native Villages*]

... Stories like this one abound and reflect the acute need for federal intervention. (62–63)

... Native Americans are the victims of crime at more than twice the rate of all U.S. residents. The rate of victimization of Native American women is 50 percent higher than the next highest group, African American males. Crimes reported in Indian Country are twice as likely to be violent in nature than are those reported in the rest of the United States.... Although the violent crime rate for Native Americans is highest in urban areas, the crime rate for rural Native Americans is more than twice that of rural whites. Moreover, Native Americans are more likely than any other racial or ethnic group to experience violence at the hands of someone of a different race....

In addition to being the victims of crime more often, Native Americans are also overrepresented in jails and prisons. American Indians are incarcerated at a rate 38 percent higher than the national per capita rate.... The number of Native American youth in the federal prison system has increased 50 percent since 1994. Many Native Americans attribute disproportionate incarceration rates to unfair treatment by the criminal justice system, including racial profiling, disparities in prosecution, and lack of access to legal representation. Because of burgeoning crime and lack of prevention programs, jails in Indian Country regularly operate beyond capacity. In 2001, the 10 largest jails were at 142 percent capacity, and nearly a third of all tribal facilities were operating above 150 percent capacity. According to a DOJ [Department of Justice] study, in some Native jails resources are so scarce that inmates do not have blankets, mattresses, or basic hygiene items, such as soap and toothpaste. (68–69)

The U.S. criminal justice system conflicts in many respects with traditional views of justice held by Native American communities. Whereas the U.S. system is based on an intricate series of laws and procedures, Native systems of justice are often guided by custom, tradition, and practices learned through the oral teachings of the elders. The goal of the Native justice system is to achieve harmony in the community and make reparations. For many Native Americans, lack of familiarity with the "foreign" and often adversarial method of justice characteristic of the federal government foster a cultural divide and further mistrust. The complexity of the jurisdictional division among federal, state, and tribal governments adds to the breakdown of law and order in Native communities. Moreover, for the law enforcement system to be effective, it must also make allowances for an intricate network of cultural and social factors. For example, alcohol and / or substance abuse borders on epidemic in Native communities, and plays a significant role in crime and victimization in Indian Country, demanding law enforcement that has corrective as well as punitive goals. (70)

The most recent studies indicate that Native American students have higher dropout rates than non-Native students. In the last decade, only 66 percent of Native American students graduated from high school, compared with 75 percent of the general population. The Commission's Montana Advisory committee studied Native American education in Montana and revealed that a decade earlier, only 23 percent of Native Americans in the state completed high school, compared with 51 percent of the general state population. In the 1994–1995 school year, Native American students dropped out of Montana high schools at a rate of 10.4 percent, 3.6 times more often than white students. In grades seven and eight, Native American students dropped out of Montana schools at a rate five times greater than their white counterparts. Taking a broader perspective, Native American students account for 3 percent of all primary and secondary dropouts nationwide despite being approximately only 1 percent of these students. (86)

Unemployment and poverty have continuously plagued the vast majority of Native American communities. On some reservations, unemployment levels have reached 85 percent. According to the 2000 census, average unemployment on reservations is 13.6 percent, more than twice the national rate. Likewise, 31.2 percent of reservation inhabitants live in poverty, and the national poverty rate for Native Americans is 24.5 percent. By contrast, the national poverty rate in the United States between 1999 and 2001 was 11.6 percent. Having reached crisis proportions, disparities in impoverishment and unemployment offer further evidence of the federal government's failure to protect the rights of and promote equal opportunities for Native Americans. (104)

Native Americans suffer food insecurity and hunger at twice the rate of the general population. USDA found that from 1995 to 1997, 22.2 percent of Native American households were food insecure, meaning they did not have enough food to meet even their basic needs. In fact, the situation was so severe that USDA determined that from 1995 to 1997, one or more members of these households suffered from moderate to severe hunger, with 8.6 percent of households experiencing both food insecurity and hunger. Among the Zuni, for example, all 2,000 children living in Zuni Pueblo are eligible for free breakfasts and lunches, with two-thirds of the reservation's inhabitants enrolled in federal food programs. (107)

According to a study of federal assistance programs for Native Americans, 45 percent of residents on three Arizona reservations in 2000–2001 indicated that they sometimes could not afford to buy food. Twenty-five percent said their children went to bed or school hungry. Seventeen percent said that in the three months prior to being interviewed there was not enough food to eat, with 3 percent saying that in those three months there was often not enough food. The stories of these Native American families and others clearly show the need for adequate FDPIR funding to provide Native Americans with enough food to meet their needs and a healthy diet available to the general population. (111)

TOPICS FOR WRITTEN OR ORAL EXPLORATION

1. List all of the crimes that are committed in *Ceremony*. In which of the crimes is alcohol a factor? Are there any crimes that you believe are morally justified?

2. Analyze how two or more of the following characters respond to alcohol: Tayo, Emo, Harley, Pinkie, Uncle Josiah. How do you account for these differences?

3. Compare the role of alcohol in this novel with the place of alcohol in literary works by other Native Americans, such as Louise Erdrich, James Welch, or Sherman Alexie.

4. Discuss the significance of alcohol in American literature generally. You might consider, for example, "The Cask of Amontillado" by Edgar Allan Poe, *The Sun Also Rises* by Ernest Hemingway, *The Great Gatsby* by F. Scott Fitzgerald, the stories of John Cheever, or *Ironweed* by William Kennedy.

5. Compare the significance of violence in *Ceremony* to that in other literature you've read, for example, *Native Son* by Richard Wright, *A Raisin in the Sun* by Lorraine Hansberry, *Waiting for the Barbarians* by J. M. Coetzee, or *Waiting* by Ha Jin.

6. Discuss stereotypes you're familiar with relating alcohol use to ethnicity. Ethnic groups you might consider include Irish, German, French, Japanese, Middle Eastern, and Russian.

7. Write a short story in which one character saves another character from some danger. The characters must be demographically different—in gender, race, ethnicity, and so forth. Most importantly, write the story without relying on or revealing any stereotypes.

8. Research the teachings of various religions (e.g., The Native American Church, Roman Catholicism, Southern Baptists, Islam, or Judaism) regarding alcohol use.

9. Survey the students at your school regarding their drug and alcohol use. Compare the results you get with those on the table of Native American youth drug and alcohol use included in this chapter.

10. Investigate programs available for treatment of addictions in your community. Organizations you might contact include AA, Narcotics Anonymous, The Betty Ford Clinic, Hazleden, and Phoenix House.

11. Research the life of Crazy Horse. Then write a letter from Crazy Horse to the Hornell Brewing Company regarding malt liquor.

12. Hold a debate in your class about the appropriate use of historical names on product labels. Does the type of product make a difference (e.g., alcohol, cigarettes, sneakers, cereal, automobiles)? Is there a difference between using the name of a real person and using a representative character (e.g., Aunt Jemima, the "Quaker" on Quaker Oats)?

13. Have you ever boycotted a product, restaurant, or store based on its name, label, advertising, or other company policies? If so, write an essay describing how and why you came to the decision you did.

14. Write an essay in which you imagine that you've been sent to a boarding school whose mission is to erase any indications of your ethnicity. How would your life be different? Consider such things as clothing and hairstyles, foods, holiday rituals, religious practices, and any other ethnic practices you can think of.

15. Plan a week's worth of nutritious meals for a family of four. Make a list of all ingredients you would need. Then visit a local grocery store as if you were shopping for those ingredients, writing down the price of each item. What would the total grocery bill be? Assume groceries account for 20 percent of a family's expenses. What is the total income a family would need to live comfortably?

16. Research the role of poverty in your city, town, or county. What are the rates of homelessness and unemployment? What is the average per capita income? How many families receive welfare assistance?

17. Interview a caseworker from your county's social services department. What must a person do to qualify for Medicaid or food stamps? How long does the application process take? What kind of documentation is necessary?

18. Relying on documents available from the U.S. Census Bureau, compare employment rates, poverty rates, or housing details in your county to similar statistics from Laguna Pueblo or from another reservation. If you live in a state with reservations, you might compare statistics between the reservations and other areas of your state.

SUGGESTED READING

Abel, Ernest L. *Fetal Alcohol Syndrome and Fetal Alcohol Effects.* New York: Plenum Press, 1987.

Berkhofer, Robert. *The White Man's Indian: Images of the American Indian from Columbus to the Present.* New York: Vintage, 1979.

Everett, Michael. *Drinking Behavior among Southwestern Indians: An Anthropological Perspective.* Albuquerque: University of Arizona Press, 1979.

French, Laurence Armand. *Addictions and Native Americans.* Westport: Praeger Press, 2000.

Hyer, Sally. *One House, One Voice, One Heart: Native American Education at the Santa Fe Indian School.* Santa Fe: Museum of New Mexico Press, 1990.

Kunitz, Stephen J., and Jerrold E. Levy. *Drinking Careers: A 25 Year Study of Three Navajo Populations.* New Haven: Yale University Press, 1994.

Kunitz, Stephen J., Jerrold E. Levy, et al. *Drinking, Conduct Disorder, and Social Change: Navajo Experiences.* New York: Oxford University Press, 2000.

Mancall, Peter C. *Deadly Medicine: Indians and Alcohol in Early America.* Ithaca: Cornell University Press, 1995.

Prucha, Francis Paul. *American Indian Policy in Crisis: Christian Reformers and the Indian, 1865–1900.* Norman: University of Oklahoma Press, 1976.

Riggs, Mary B. *Early Days at Santee: The Beginnings of Santee Normal Training School.* Santee: Santee N.T.S. Press, 1928.

Shkilnyk, Anastasia M. *A Poison Stronger Than Love.* New Haven: Yale University Press, 1985.

Streissguth, Ann Pytkowicz. *A Manual on Adolescents and Adults with Fetal Alcohol Syndrome with Special Reference to American Indians.* Washington: Indian Health Service, 1986.

Thomason, Timothy C. "Issues in the Treatment of Native Americans with Alcohol Problems." *Journal of Multicultural Counseling and Development.* (October 2000): 243–52.

Trennert, Robert A., Jr. *The Phoenix Indian School: Forced Assimilation in Arizona, 1891–1935.* Norman: University of Oklahoma Press, 1988.

Unrau, William E., ed. *White Man's Wicked Water: The Alcohol Trade and Prohibition in Indian Country.* Lawrence: University of Kansas Press, 1996.

Waddell, Jack O., and Michael W. Everett, eds. *Drinking Behavior among Southwestern Indians: An Anthropological Perspective.* Tucson: University of Arizona Press, 1980.

Index

About the Author

LYNN DOMINA is Associate Professor of English at the State University of New York, Delhi, where her research focuses on Native American and African-American Literature. She is the author of a book of poetry, *Corporal Works,* and *Understanding* A Raisin in the Sun (Greenwood, 1993).